THE GENDER OF ROSALIND

Jan Kott

THE GENDER OF ROSALIND

Interpretations: Shakespeare,
Büchner, Gautier

Translated by Jadwiga Kosicka
and Mark Rosenzweig

NORTHWESTERN UNIVERSITY PRESS
EVANSTON, ILLINOIS

Northwestern University Press
Evanston, Illinois 60201

Printed in the United States of America

ISBN: 0-8101-1013-X (cloth)
        0-8101-1038-5 (paper)

Library of Congress Cataloging-in-Publication Data
Kott, Jan.
   The gender of Rosalind : interpretations : Shakespeare, Büchner,
Gautier / Jan Kott ; translated by Jadwiga Kosicka and Mark
Rosenzweig.
      p.   cm.
   Collection of essays, by the author, translated from the Polish.
   Includes index.
   ISBN 0-8101-1013-X (alk. paper);   0-8101-1038-5 (pbk.)
      1. Shakespeare, William, 1564–1616—Criticism and interpretation.
   2. Rosalind (Fictitious character)
PR2976.K67   1992
822.3'3—dc20   91-33301
                                                           CIP

The paper used in this publication meets the minimum requirements of
American National Standard for Information Sciences—Permanence of
Paper for Printed Library Materials, ANSI Z39.48-1984.

To my grandson, Matthew

Contents

Acknowledgments

The essays collected in *The Gender of Rosalind* were revised from the following original publications and are used here with permission: "The Gender of Rosalind," from *New Theatre Quarterly*; "Head for Maidenhead, Maidenhead for Head," from *Theatre Quarterly*; and "The Guillotine as a Tragic Hero," from *The New York Review of Books*.

INTRODUCTION

Still Contemporary?

T he place is the rocky shore of Jersey, one of the Chan-
nel Islands off the coast of Normandy, closer to France
than to England and almost at the point where La
Manche joins the Atlantic Ocean. The time is a wintry night;
the high waves crash against the shore. Slowly, braving the
blowing wind, two men walk toward the beach. A father and
son.

"What do you think of this exile?" asked the younger man.

"That it will be long," said the elder, who resembled a lion.

After a moment of silence, the son again questioned his father: "How do you expect to fill the time?"

"I shall gaze at the ocean," the father replied. Another pro-
longed silence. "And you?" the father resumed.

"I shall translate Shakespeare," said the son.

This conversation took place in the early 1850s. The older
man was Victor Hugo, the younger, his son François-Victor,
the best translator of Shakespeare in nineteenth-century France.
In this conversation, recorded by Victor in his *William Shakespeare* (1864), the ocean and Shakespeare were somehow
equated.[1] The ocean is beyond human time, or rather it

encompasses a multitude of human times, and only one of them is the "present"—and then only when we look at it. Sometimes this "present" is long; for Victor Hugo it stretched out into nineteen years of exile after he had refused to support Napoleon III's coup d'état. The time of exile is one of the many "times" in which *The Winter's Tale* and *The Tempest* may appear most striking.

Shakespeare had already become "contemporary" during the Restoration when his plays were freely adapted and altered to suit the crude taste of the time for the sensational, and he is "contemporary" in the no less ruthless "tryouts" and workshops by directors during the past quarter century. Shakespeare has been and continues to be a mirror of the time.

As in Orwell's *Animal Farm,* where all the animals are equal but some are more equal than others, Shakespeare in some periods was more contemporary than in others, but in no period was he more contemporary than during the Romantic rebellion for George Sand and Mérimée, Alfred de Vigny and Gautier, Stendhal and Musset in France, for Kleist and Büchner in Germany, for Malczewski, Mickiewicz, and Słowacki in Poland, for Pushkin in Russia. And most of all for Victor Hugo.

In the preface to *Cromwell* (1827), the manifesto of Romantic drama, Hugo wrote: "This Melpomene, as she is called, would shudder at the thought of touching a chronicle. She leaves the knowledge of the epic she is evoking to the care of the costume designer. To her mind, history is ill bred and in bad taste. How is it possible, for example, to tolerate kings and queens who curse?"[2]

In all branches of art, being contemporary means the choice of tradition, but nowhere is this more true than in the theater. Being contemporary is the choice of one past as a model rather than other pasts and other models. Victor Hugo and French Romantics chose Shakespeare as their patron rather than Racine, who was for them *la vieux perruque.* For his drama about

Danton Büchner found the model of historical tragedy in Shakespeare's *Julius Caesar* as opposed to Schiller, who considered Shakespeare's play a parade of affected and pathetic marionettes, not a "true history." Mickiewicz ridiculed the Warsaw classicists for whom pastoral poetry was the "true history" and took Hamlet's "there are more things in heaven and earth, Horatio, / than are dreamt of in your philosophy" as the motto for his *Forefathers' Eve,* the masterpiece of Polish Romantic drama.

There are always two times in the theater: the time of the spectator, which continues to exist even when the lights go out, and the time or even the many rapidly changing times onstage. The contemporary, the con-temporary, is the interconnection between these two times: "they [the players] are the abstract and brief chronicles of the time" (*Hamlet* II.ii.520).[3] In Hamlet's speech to Polonius, *time* is the most important word. For Shakespeare it was the time of his audiences attending productions of his plays: noblemen and princesses at the court theater, burghers and whores at the Globe. But what image of what time and what chronicle of what "true history" are offered to us by the actors of our time? Spectators must see their own image in the actors. In *Wilhelm Meisters Lehrjahre* Goethe sees Hamlet as "a lovely, pure, noble and most moral nature, without the strength of nerve which forms a hero, [that] sinks beneath a burden which it cannot bear and must not cast away. All duties are holy to him; the present is too hard."[4] *Present* is the most important word here.

What was the present for that German Hamlet in 1795, three years after the guillotining of Louis XVI, one year after Danton's execution, and several months after Robespierre's fall? In France the Reign of Terror was about to end. Germany was still divided into at least two hundred petty and grand duchies and electorates. Goethe was forty-eight years old; Kleist was twenty-two. A new generation of twenty year olds was coming of age, a generation of idealists and dreamers brought up on

Kant and Fichte, rebels who lacked the strength to rebel. The Prince of Homburg, the protagonist of Kleist's play of the same name, perhaps the best and at the same time the most ambiguous drama of German Romanticism, is, like Goethe's Hamlet, inwardly split and because of his nobility totally lost in the brutal world once he awakens from his dream.

Brecht's German Hamlet is different. In the *Kleines Organon für das Theater* (1948), Brecht wrote: "The theatre has to speak up decisively for the interests of its own time. Let us take as an example . . . the old play *Hamlet*. Given the dark and bloody time. . . ." The key word *time*—his time and ours—appears again. "Given the dark and bloody time in which I am writing—the criminal ruling classes, the widespread doubt in the power of reason, continually being misused—I think that I can read the story thus: It is an age of warriors. . . . Fortinbras is arming for . . . a predatory war against Poland. . . . he [Hamlet] meets young Fortinbras at the coast as he is marching with his troops to Poland."[5]

I doubt that ever before had any summary of *Hamlet* put Poland so much in the forefront. But when Brecht wrote at that "dark and bloody time," some three years after the Yalta agreement, Europe was already divided into two blocs, and Poland had been consigned to subjugation by the Soviet Union. "Overcome by this warrior-like example, he turns back and in a piece of barbaric butchery slaughters his uncle, his mother and himself, leaving Denmark to the Norwegian." "Leaving Denmark to the Norwegian"—Brecht's reading of the denouement of *Hamlet* is as startling as his mention of Poland a few sentences earlier. "These events show the young man, already somehow stout, making the most ineffective use of the new approach to Reason which he has picked up at the university of Wittenberg. In the feudal business to which he returns it simply hampers him. Faced with irrational practices, his reason is utterly impractical. He falls a tragic victim to the discrepancy between such reasoning and such action."[6]

Brecht knew Goethe by heart, of course. But it is startling that 150 years after Goethe and 3 years after the end of the Second World War the present is as "hard" for this German Hamlet. Goethe's opposition between the nobility of Hamlet's nature and the inexorability of vengeance becomes in Brecht a contrast between the University of Wittenberg and feudal Elsinore, a feudal Elsinore as bloody and barbaric as Hitler's Germany. And once again the present invaded the Shakespearean stage.

My book *Shakespeare Our Contemporary* had its origins in a production of *Hamlet* that I saw in Kraków in September 1956.[7] I called it "*Hamlet* after the Twentieth Congress." At that congress of the Communist party in Moscow, Khrushchev delivered his famous "secret" speech denouncing Stalin's crimes. This new Kraków Hamlet was wearing jeans and was an "angry young man," as were his peers in the Western countries. He had just returned from existential Wittenberg to Communist Elsinore. For the third time this inwardly split Hamlet became the victim of contradictions between Sartre's inner freedom and the unconditional morality of rebellion.

In 1956 Adam Michnik was barely ten years old. A few years later, just as the first edition of *Shakespeare Our Contemporary* came out in Poland, Adam and his friends organized the Club of Contradiction Seekers at the high school they attended. Orthodox party bureaucrats called them "revisionists crawling on all fours." The word *dissident* was not yet known in Poland at the time.

When during the past year or two I lectured to students at both American and Polish universities, I began to realize that the majority of my listeners had not yet been born when I was working on *Shakespeare Our Contemporary*. If that Shakespeare was contemporary in the sixties, can he be contemporary now?

That, of course, was a Shakespeare imbued with politics, a Shakespeare coming after the Hitler nightmare and after the funeral of Stalin, whose coffin had been borne on the shoulders of Malenkov, Bulganin, Beria, and Khrushchev, all wearing huge fur hats. Beria was executed, and all the others in due succession fell from the heights of power into oblivion, Khrushchev being the last in the line. In *Shakespeare Our Contemporary* I tried to show how the Wheel of Fortune of the Greco-Roman and medieval traditions was now being turned not by Fate but by the winds of history. I called it the Grand Mechanism.

This Shakespeare of mine from a quarter century ago, however, was not only political. It was also an attempt to recognize a new dramatic method and point it out to the theaters of our time. Victor Hugo's Romantic theater and Brecht's epic theater found their model in Shakespeare. In this theatrical dialectic both Victor Hugo's and Brecht's theater took a new look at Shakespeare's stage. And not only Brecht, Beckett, and Genet can be traced to Shakespeare. In the late 1960s and early 1970s the theater of the absurd became an unexpected ally of the new "contemporary" Shakespeare. Peter Brook's *King Lear* and *A Midsummer Night's Dream,* the history plays under Peter Hall's direction, Giorgio Strehler's *The Tempest,* and Peter Stein's Berlin production of *As You Like It* were not only a revival of Shakespeare, not only Shakespeare "our contemporary," but a revival of the theater itself, making it "our contemporary theater."

Every era has the Shakespeare it deserves, or at least each theater has the Shakespeare it deserves. It appears that this extraordinary connection between Shakespeare and contemporary drama and theater, which occurred at least twice since the time of the Romantic revolt, has already passed. Shakespeare has ceased to be the discovery of any new theater, and the theater for almost the past twenty years has not been the discovery of a new contemporary Shakespeare.

If Shakespeare has ceased to be "contemporary," as he was in the sixties, he has become as never before a universal Shakespeare. His plays are staged all over the world: in India, Japan, and China, in Europe from Madrid to Omsk in Siberia, and in the Americas. At Stratford-upon-Avon and Stratford, Ontario, Shakespearean productions are no less artistic events than unfailing tourist attractions. Even on Broadway Shakespeare for tourists is a new universal Shakespeare.

In the already quoted preface to *Cromwell* Hugo wrote about Melpomene, who entrusted the costume designer with such cares as the time and place of a drama. In the past two decades it is the hairdresser, the electrician, and the tailor who give a modern look to Shakespeare. As do none of the other great playwrights, Shakespeare simply asks for purely theatrical stagings. His plays can be staged in historical or fantastic costumes, with scenery that can be a painstaking re-creation of the Roman Forum or on a bare stage, in the nude or almost in the nude (as in productions I have seen in Edinburgh and Berlin), or, what has already become a new style in England, in an astonishing eclecticism of dress. In a production of *The Tempest,* on Prospero's "bare island" Miranda wearing only a bra greets the royal entourage decked out in Renaissance costumes. Ariane Mnouchkine's productions of the history plays were presented in a simulated Kabuki style, with the kings and courtiers dressed in samurai costumes.

In this new universal Shakespeare not only are costumes haphazardly mixed, but so are all languages and theatrical styles. In the nineteenth century Shakespeare's plays were frequently, and with great success, made into opera librettos. Today the most accessible and universal Shakespeare appears on film and television. In these new hybrids Shakespearean dialogue acquires a new and sharper relevance in the modern world. In Kurosawa's *Throne of Blood,* the Japanese Macbeth dies like a giant hedgehog, pinned with arrows to the door of his castle. Kurosawa's *Ran,* based on *King Lear,* ends in a long shot of the sky filled with black clouds and the fields laid waste, with no trace left of the castles over which the war had been waged. In medieval Japan, torn apart by warring feudal clans, Kurosawa discovered a Shakespearean cruelty and at the same time a rigor of gesture that the Anglo-Saxon theater in its quest for novelty seems to have forgotten. Surprisingly, in a series of unexpected affinities, Kenneth Branagh's cinematic version of *Henry V* has a daring similar to that of Kurosawa's films. The contemporary for us lies not in the appearances and falsity of costume but in the tyranny of rulers and the cruelty of war, vividly shown at Agincourt, where in the fog and whirling clouds bodies lie entwined in the mud mixed with blood.

Like the ocean that Victor Hugo and his son looked at during long years of exile, all Shakespearean times in every stage version, but even more in every film adaptation, become interconnected: the historical Shakespeare, the contemporary Shakespeare, the universal Shakespeare. Although a new drama is lacking that could serve as a mirror to reflect Shakespeare, the contemporary is always present in the actor's body, in his voice and in his gaze.

Not long ago we saw on our television screens the huge crowds in front of the Central Committee in Bucharest howling "A rat! A rat!" when they saw the helicopter with Ceauşescu take off from the roof of the presidential palace, and a day later Ceauşescu was being pulled up by the neck like a huge rat from the bottom of a tank. Before our very eyes the Grand Mechanism was being replayed in history once again.

If the theater balks at the return of political Shakespeare, the urgency of politics comes back to the public square in the turns and twists of history and from there finds its way to our eyes and ears.

Notes

1. Victor Hugo, *William Shakespeare* (Paris, 1965).

2. Victor Hugo, "Preface to *Cromwell* (1827)," trans. Barry Daniels, in *Revolution in the Theatre* (Westport, Conn., 1959).

3. Quotations of *Hamlet* are from the Arden Shakespeare edition, ed. Harold Jenkins (London, 1982).

4. J. W. von Goethe, *Wilhelm Meister's Apprenticeship,* trans. Thomas Carlyle, 2 vols. (Boston, 1901).

5. Bertolt Brecht, *Brecht on Theatre,* trans. John Willett (New York, 1964), 201–2.

6. Ibid.

7. Jan Kott, *Shakespeare Our Contemporary* (New York, 1964).

Translated by Jadwiga Kosicka

THE GENDER OF
ROSALIND

On the Elizabethan stage the roles of young girls and even mature women were played by fourteen- or fifteen-year-old boys, always of course before their voices changed. The boy actor must have been like the *onnagata* in the traditional Kabuki. In the Japanese theater the convention is never bared onstage or the illusion abruptly suspended. In Shakespeare's theater, however, at least on two occasions the convention is suddenly unveiled for a brief moment; dramatic illusion is transformed into "theater in the theater," and as in Brecht's alienation effect theatrical time for that moment becomes audience time, and the performer who represents the role is not the he, or, rather, the she, whose role is being played.

In a dazzling Shakespearean anachronism, Cleopatra, queen of Egypt and mistress of Roman emperors, has no sooner ordered her maid to undo her bodice than she becomes for a moment a squeaking boy:

> the quick comedians
> Extemporally will stage us . . .
> . . . Antony
> Shall be brought drunken forth, and I shall see
> Some squeaking Cleopatra boy my greatness
> I' the posture of a whore.
> (*Antony and Cleopatra* V.ii.215–20)[1]

In the final scene of *As You Like It,* a boy who played a girl, who in turn played herself disguised as a boy, took off the doublet and hose tightly fastened around the knees. In the epilogue, back in women's clothes, Rosalind speaks directly to the spectators: "It is not the fashion to see the lady the epilogue; but it is no more unhandsome than to see the lord the prologue. . . . If I were a woman I would kiss as many of you as had beards that pleased me, complexions that liked me, and breaths that I defied not: and I am sure, as many . . . will, for my kind offer, when I make curtsy, bid me farewell."

"If I were a woman"—but now Rosalind not only wears a long gown that sweeps the ground and an ample bodice, but she curtsies as she leaves the stage. Genet insisted that at every performance of his *Blacks,* if there were no white spectators, a black in a white mask should be seated in the front row. The court consists of white judges only, but in fact they are blacks in white masks. "But what exactly is a black?" Genet asks. "First of all what's his color?"[2] We could rephrase Genet and ask: "What exactly is gender? And above all, what's gender of gender?" In *A Natural Perspective,* essays on Shakespearean comedy and romance, Northrop Frye made a most penetrating observation on the links between reality and illusion onstage: "In watching tragedy we are impressed by the reality of the illusion. . . . In watching romantic comedy we are impressed by the illusion of the reality."[3] The stage is both the reality of the illusion and the illusion of the reality. Following Frye, we could say: The illusion of gender is the gender of illusion. A girl/boy is a boy/girl. But what is his/her gender?

2

In a half-dozen Shakespearean comedies a youthful actor whose face has yet to feel the razor plays a girl who adopts the disguise of a boy. But in at least two masterpieces of Shakespearean comedy the disguise is not only a convention that serves to tie and untie the love intrigue. In such sparkling allegros with seemingly happy denouements as *Twelfth Night* and *As You Like It*, the ambiguity of gender is a bitter and truly disturbing theme not fully brought to light and still to be dealt with by the theater.

In the second scene of *Twelfth Night*, soon after coming ashore on the seacoast of Illyria, Viola says:

> Thou shalt present me as an eunuch to him.
> .... for I can sing,
> And speak to him in many sorts of music
> That will allow me very worth his service.
> (I.ii.56–59)

Not long ago some Shakespeare scholars suggested that at one point Viola was to sing the songs eventually given to the clown Feste. But in the passage cited above Shakespeare used the blunt word *eunuch*, not *singer*. A few lines later he repeated it in the speech of the Sea Captain, Viola's friend: "Be you his eunuch, and your mute I'll be" (II.ii.62).

There are no random words in Shakespeare, especially words like *eunuch*, so jarring to poetic diction. In an ambiguous confession, Viola, who has become Cesario, says: "Disguise, I see thou art a wickedness / Wherein the pregnant enemy does much" (II.ii.26–27). Christian anthropology teaches that man has one soul and one body. Disguise as another body is a sin, hence the condemnation of theater since the days of Tertullian and Origen. One body and one sex. Playing the opposite sex is temptation by the devil: "How will this fadge? My master loves her dearly, / And I, poor monster . . ." (II.ii.32–33).

"And I, poor monster"—legendary and mythological monsters defy classification; they combine a lion's head with a woman's torso and an eagle's wings, or a woman's torso with a bird's beak. The eunuch and the hermaphrodite are "monsters" too. The hermaphrodite is an anatomical mediation between the male and female bodies. The androgyne was a platonic mediation in the Florentine and Elizabethan neoplatonic tradition:

> As I am man,
> My state is desperate for my master's love:
> As I am woman (now alas the day!)
> What thriftless sighs shall poor Olivia breathe?
>
> (II.ii.36–39)

The boy/girl appears as a fascination/obsession in almost the same words in *As You Like It*, the *Sonnets*, and *Twelfth Night*, subtitled *What You Will*. What you will? "I am all the daughters of my father's house, / And all the brothers too" (II.iv.121–22). The Duke says to Viola/Cesario:

> Diana's lip
> Is not more smooth and rubious: thy small pipe
> Is as the maiden's organ, shrill and sound,
> And all is semblative a woman's part.
>
> (I.iv.31–34)[4]

Malvolio says of the Duke's messenger: "Not yet old enough for a man, nor young enough for a boy: as a squash is before 'tis a peascod, or a codling when 'tis almost an apple. 'Tis with him in standing water, between boy and man" (I.v.158–61).

"I am not that I play," says the boy/girl to Olivia during their first meeting. But even more characteristic is what Olivia says to herself: "Methinks I feel this youth's perfections" (I.v.300).[5] In botany the perfect flower has both stamens and pistils (male and female reproductive organs respectively). Perfection in the sense of sexual ambivalence is perfection for the followers of Sappho. At her next meeting with Olivia, Viola/Cesario will be transformed into Sebastian. The theme of siblings lost at sea and miraculously reunited, repeated in countless versions in comedies and romances from antiquity through the late Middle Ages, the Renaissance, and even the age of the baroque, is borrowed by Shakespeare from Plautus's *Menaechmi* for *The Comedy of Errors.* But in *Twelfth Night* in a brilliant reversal of gender, the twins are brother and sister, man and woman. The stamen and pistil are doubles, not to be told apart by their love partners: "One face, one voice, one habit, and two persons! / A natural perspective, that is, and is not!" (V.i.214–15). Antonio, Sebastian's friend and the ship's second captain during that night of mirrored errors, will repeat after the Duke: "An apple cleft in two is not more twin / Than these two creatures. Which is Sebastian?" (V.i.221–22).[6]

For the first and only time, Viola/Cesario and Sebastian are separated in the final scene of the play. They are to be separated as they appear together onstage. In accord with the tradition and rules of the genre, the romantic plot of the comedy ends in a "happy" joining of the two couples. Cesario, detached from Viola, has become Sebastian. But Viola and Sebastian are doubles. The girl/boy and the boy/girl will never stop circling between the Duke and Olivia like wooden horses on a merry-go-round during that "twelfth" night that never ends.

The Duke's final words about this night of mistaken identities are as brutal as those at the very beginning when Viola is to adopt the role of a eunuch. Viola is still in britches and doublet.

> Cesario, come;
> For so you shall be while you are a man;
> But when in other habits you are seen,
> Orsino's mistress, and his fancy's queen.
>
> (V.i.384–87)

In Elizabethan idiom this Shakespearean text (as well as a passage in the final scene of *The Merchant of Venice*) is almost openly obscene: "Orsino's mistress, and his fancy's queen." A "fancy woman" meant a kept woman or, in slang, a harlot, whore, strumpet (*Webster's*). A "fancy man" meant lover and, more frequently, a harlot protector (*Webster's* and the *O.E.D.*). But what exactly is "fancy's queen"? In French argot it is *reine*, in Italian *regina*; in England from the Elizabethan period until the present day and in America, a "queen" is a man in drag.[7]

Sheridan Square on the Lower East Side of Manhattan is the site of an annual Halloween gay parade. The "queens" appear wearing monstrously big padded bras and enormous green, red, or purple wigs, their hair braided or pinned up into "cocks' combs." Alongside those frightening male/female figures resembling gigantic ostriches or parrots with hooked beaks, there are groups of boy/girls with hair cut short, either half-naked or in long, transparent gowns, dancing or holding hands, who look like angels in Pre-Raphaelite paintings.[8] Angels are genderless. But Satan does show gender even in disguise: "Disguise, I see thou art a wickedness" (II.ii.26).

3

In *Twelfth Night* the triangle of Shakespearean eros almost graphically shapes the action and the relations between the characters. Viola/Cesario and her/his double, Sebastian, are the base of this triangle. The Duke, Orsino, is its left side, Olivia its right. The two symmetric ship captains, Viola's "mute" admirer and Antonio desperately searching for Viola's brother throughout Illyria, can be added to the triangle's two bottom vertices.

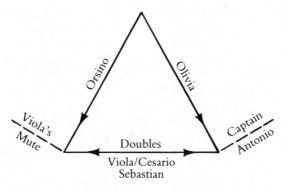

The love relationship without disguise, between man and woman, between Orsino and Olivia, is frozen; Olivia hides her passion under courtly manners, and Orsino hides his under the cold rhetoric of baroque concepts. From the very start the pulsation of eros is felt only between the Duke and the boy inherent in the girl, and between Olivia and the girl inherent in the boy. Instinct and sexual choices are not deluded by disguise, as if Shakespeare knew that he was only concealing and finding his own excuses for the inversions of desire. In a mask or a domino, sexual aggression and provocation elude social restraint and even one's own self-censorship. Disguise not only covers but also uncovers and bares.

The same triangle of Shakespearean eros is repeated in the *Sonnets*. The man, the "I" of the *Sonnets*, is its left side. The Dark Lady, who "would corrupt my saint to be a devil" (144.7) and took the youth away, is its right side. In the *Sonnets* the youth, "the better, fair angel," is the base of the triangle:

> Two loves I have, of comfort and despair:
> Which like two spirits do suggest me still.
> The better angel is a man right fair.
>
> (144.1–3)

In Marlowe's *Edward II* this youth is "in Dian's shape." In the *Sonnets* he has the face of a woman: "On Helen's cheek all art beauty set, / And you in Grecian tires are painted new" (53.7–8). Like "Orsino's mistress" in *Twelfth Night*, "the master mistress of my passion" in the *Sonnets* is an androgyne: "A woman's face, with Nature's own hand painted / Hast thou, the master mistress of my passion" (20.1–2).

The triangle from the *Sonnets* is repeated in *As You Like It*. Orlando is its left side, Phebe its right (in a certain sense Celia is the right side at the beginning of the action). But its sides do not close. There is no discernible eros between Orlando and Phebe or between Orlando and Celia (or perhaps only in a substitute form, since Orlando's brother marries Celia in the traditional comedic ending). The base of the triangle in *As You Like It* is Rosalind/Ganymede, the most fascinating and disturbing of all of Shakespeare's boy/girls both in the reading and on the stage:

> CELIA: What shall I call thee when thou art a man?
> ROSALIND: I'll have no worse a name than Jove's own page,
> And, therefore, look you call me Ganymede.
> (I.iii.125–27)

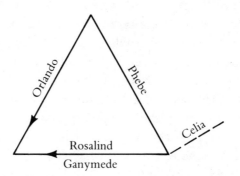

The source of Shakespeare's *As You Like It* is Thomas Lodge's pastoral romance *Rosalynde* (1590), in which the daughter of a banished prince, driven out by the usurper to the throne, escapes with her female cousin to the Forest of Arden. Shakespeare took from Lodge not only the main line of the plot but also the sexually double name Rosalynde/Ganymede. The amazing peculiarity of that pastoral idyll is the deliberate and constant interchange of the pronouns *she, he, her,* and *his* throughout the story as if Lodge wanted to remind us that "she" (Rosalynde) is a woman, and "he" (Ganymede) is a man.[9] But Rosalynde/Ganymede is one person. The alternation of pronouns on the level of the text is grammar of the androgyne.

Ganymede is not only a meaningful name, but from antiquity through the Renaissance and up to the late eighteenth century it was univocal. It meant a male lover. The "amorous girl-boy," as Lodge called him, reappears in Marlowe's poem *Hero and Leander*, written at almost the same period as *As You Like It:*

> Some swore he was a maid in mans attire,
> For in his lookes were all that men desire,
> . . . .
> *Jove,* slylie stealing from his sisters bed
> To dallie with *Idalian Ganimed.*[10]

Before Rosalind, back in woman's clothes, is united with Orlando in a marriage ceremony during the last scene of the comedy, however, she will go through love games involving both her sexes, male and female, and through a parody of a wedding ritual that almost anticipates Genet. While still at the Duke's court, before her banishment and subsequent transformation into a boy, she experienced the first girlish stirrings of emotion with her cousin Celia: "whose loves / Are dearer than the natural bond of sisters" (I.ii.87–88).

In Peter Stein's critically acclaimed production of *As You Like It* at the Berlin Schausbühne in the late 1980s, Celia and her "sweet girl" in man's attire pursued their amorous game in the thickets of the Forest of Arden almost to the very end of this comedy of disguise. Celia, now as Aliena, says:

> We still have slept together,
> Rose at an instant, learn'd, play'd, eat together;
> And whersoe'er we went, like Juno's swans,
> Still we went coupled and inseparable.
>
> (I.iii.76–79)

In that love dearer than "the natural bond of sisters," Celia had said to her "sweet girl":

> Thou and I am one;
> Shall we be sunder'd? shall we part . . .
> . . . .
> Say what thou canst, I'll go along with thee.
>
> (I.iii.96–97, 104)

In the Forest of Arden Celia is called Aliena and both as a sister and as an alien accompanies Rosalind throughout her experiences as Ganymede. But in disguise Rosalind is also an alien, not only for Phebe and unrecognized by Orlando, but for herself suddenly estranged like one's face reflected in the mirror which is I and not I. She is in the mirror but also outside it. Rosalind sees another face, the face of the opposite sex: "Alas the day! what shall I do with my doublet and hose?" (III.ii.221). And like Viola: "I am not that I play." Rosalind tries to convince Aliena as well as herself: "Do you not know I am a woman?" (III.ii.263).

The Forest of Arden is an initiation into eros. But like the process of maturing, it proves to be yet another encounter with the mirror in which desire for the other is reflected as a premonition of one's own sexuality: "this shepherd's passion / Is much upon my fashion." (II.iv.61–62). A shepherd's? For a moment Rosalind finds herself in Silvius as he sighs for Phebe:

> The sight of lovers feedeth those in love.
> Bring us unto this sight, and you shall say
> I'll prove a busy actor in their play.
>
> (III.iv.52–54)

In his brilliant preface to Genet's *The Maids*, where the sexes are interchanged, Sartre writes that the actor in order to be "true" must be false to himself—false to his gender in Genet's erotics.[11] But for a transvestite the false gender is his truth. In the "play" in which Rosalind is to appear the "busy actor" is Ganymede. In the Forest of Arden Rosalind is not as in contemporary theater a woman ineptly disguised as a man, but Ganymede: "I pray you, do not fall in love with me, / For I am falser than vows made in wine" (III.v.57–58). Phebe too is a false shepherdess. In that "forest" entered directly from a princely court, Phebe like Olivia in *Twelfth Night* and the "bad angel" in the *Sonnets* desires a girlish youth. In all his physical beauty, in all his undisguised corporeality,

His leg is but so-so; and yet 'tis well:
There was a pretty redness in his lip;
A little riper and more lusty red
Than that mix'd in his cheek; t'was just the difference
Betwixt the constant red and mingled damask.

(III.v.116–20)

The perseveration of the symbolic opposition of colors is astonishing. In the erotic triangle Phebe has replaced the Dark Lady. Her hair too is black:

'Tis not your inky brows, your black silk hair,
Your bugle eyeballs, nor your cheek of cream,
That can entame my spirits to your worship.

(III.v.44–46)

Fascination continues: "Sweet youth, I pray you chide a year together" (III.v.64).

The deception is mutual: the deceived is also the deceiver. In the Forest of Arden and in each and every Illyria not only genders are disguised; sex itself is in disguise. Lesbos is unfulfilled, but desire even if unsatisfied never ceases to feed the imagination. In *Sodome et Gomorrhe* Proust writes: "The young man whom we have been attempting to portray was so evidently a woman that the women who looked upon him with desire were doomed (failing a special taste on their part) to the same disappointment as those who in Shakespeare's comedies are taken in by a girl disguised as a youth. The deception is mutual, the invert is himself aware of it, he guesses the disillusionment which the woman will experience once the mask is removed, and feels to what an extent this mistake as to sex is a source of poetical imaginings."[12] Rosalind, now a "busy actor" in short breeches and brightly colored hose, will test her new charms: "I will speak to him like a saucy lacquey, and under that habit play the knave with him" (III.ii.313).

Yet in the night of beautiful people in drag, Ganymede wants enamored Orlando to woo him not as a boy, but as Rosalind:

> ORLANDO: I would not be cured, youth
> ROSALIND: I would cure you if you would but call me Rosalind,
> and come every day to my cote and woo me.
> . . . .
> ORLANDO: With all my heart, good youth.
> ROSALIND: Nay, you must call me Rosalind.
>
> (III.ii.446)

As You Like It has two different endings: a happy ending that resolves the conflicts according to the rules and conventions of comedy, in which the Duke returns from the banishment, the good and bad brothers are reconciled, and Hymen unites the loving couples. But earlier in the play, there is another ending in which Ganymede is the bride. Everyone is disguised by this point, not only Touchstone (a clown is always disguised) but also Celia/Aliena, who has to play the role of priest in this fake ritual that takes place on the fragile boundary between carnival and blasphemy:

> ROSALIND: Come, sister, you shall be the priest and
> marry us.—Give me your hand, Orlando:—What do
> you say, sister?
> ORLANDO: Pray thee marry us.
> CELIA: I cannot say the words.
> ROSALIND: You must begin,—"Will you, Orlando,—"
> CELIA: Go to:—Will you, Orlando, have to wife this Rosalind?
>
> (IV.i.124)

Desire and its disappointments, disguise and bodies in disguise, gender and illusions of gender are all intermingled and seem interchangeable. Silvius looks fondly at Phebe, Phebe looks fondly at Ganymede, Ganymede looks fondly at Orlando; Orlando loves Rosalind, Rosalind is Ganymede. In the Elizabethan theater where young boys were Rosalind/Ganymede, Phebe the shepherdess infatuated with Ganymede, and Celia/Aliena who plays the priest, the confusion of gender must have been total.[13] But how can this confusion be shown and made convincing in the contemporary theater on both sides of the Atlantic that has neither the Japanese *onnagata* nor the boy actors up to such a task?

But there are other possible models. More than twenty years ago while I was still working on *Shakespeare Our Contemporary*, I spent one cold winter night in a discotheque in Stockholm. When the deafening music and frenetic dancing stopped for a moment and the blinding lights ceased whirling, the dancers would slowly leave the dance floor, their bodies still swaying rhythmically, and move toward the walls locked in each other's arms. They stood there for a long time oblivious to everything around them. All of them had blond hair closely cropped at the nape of the neck and were tall and long-legged, in tightly fitting jeans and loose denim jackets—boys and girls, girls and boys, indistinguishable one from the other. After a while a pair of dancers pried themselves from the wall and came over to the Swedish friends I was with. They were both female; on their jackets they had the identifying mark GIRL embroidered in red. It seems to me that in *Twelfth Night* the roles of the doubles, Viola/Cesario and Sebastian, should be played by two women disguised as men, instead of by an actor and actress. A young woman whose body is not fully developed is closer in appearance to an androgyne than a man. But in a new Elizabethan production of *As You Like It*, what should be the gender of the person playing Rosalind/Ganymede?

4

In his *Mademoiselle de Maupin* (1835), Gautier was the first of the young Romantics to describe with the passion of a true neophyte the ambivalence of desire. But the novel's most astonishing innovation is the amateur production of *As You Like It*, played not to reveal the gender of Shakespeare's Rosalind, but as a test for discovering the gender of the performer of the role. The new Mademoiselle de Maupin played Rosalind in this ingenious production, proving that Gautier possessed theatrical imagination of which Shakespeare experts and theater scholars could be envious.

Before entering legend, Mademoiselle de Maupin was a real historic figure. She lived at the end of the seventeenth century. Always dressed in men's attire, an excellent equestrienne, and known for her courage as a duelist, she had many lovers of both sexes. She is said to have been the first contralto heard on the Paris operatic stage, appearing triumphantly in *Tancred*.

Gautier was only twenty-four when *Mademoiselle de Maupin* was published. Chevalier D'Albert, the novel's protagonist and narrator in most of the chapters, is the same age as Gautier and appears to be an alter ego of the author's, revealing his sexual fantasies. As the novel opens, D'Albert meets a young widow in a rose-colored gown in one of the salons. Rosette (she appears in the novel under this name) invites D'Albert to her country estate. Time in the novel is fluid. At the beginning it seems to be a contemporary novel, then the action appears to switch to the palaces and gardens typical of eighteenth-century libertine novels. The clothing of the "widow in rose," especially her lingerie and peignoirs, come from the Regency era. The scenery of the novel is a park, a forest, and a boudoir.

Despite the lovers' inventiveness in ever new and varied sexual pleasures, D'Albert's erotic imagination remains ungratified. Nurtured on Greek myth, it may appear contrived. But in the human soul-trapped-in-body the imagination too is carnal and feeds on its own sensual needs, be they concealed, partially avowed, or slowly penetrating to full awareness. "There is scarcely any difference between Paris and Helen."[14] They are more tellingly and openly expressed in another of D'Albert's confessions: "This son of Hermes and Aphrodite is, in fact, one of the sweetest creations of Pagan genius. Nothing in the world can be imagined more ravishing than these two bodies, harmoniously blended together and both perfect, these two beauties so equal and so different, forming but one superior to both." In this Romantic novel Gautier is amazingly modern in his evocation of sexual transgression: "I have never wished so much for anything as, like Tiresias the soothsayer, to meet on the mountain the serpents which cause the change of sex, and what I envy most in the monstrous and whimsical gods of India are their perpetual *avatars* and their countless transformations."

D'Albert would like to change into his love partner in order to experience female eros: "I would have preferred to be a woman. . . . I would willingly have changed my part, for it is very provoking to be unaware of the effect that one produces, and to judge of the enjoyment of others only by one's own." In this eros of the imagination, the hermaphrodite is not only a joining of the two split halves from the platonic myth in the *Symposium*, but a fulfillment of the impossible desire that during the act of love the male could become female and the female male.

These phantasms become embodied with the arrival of Théodore, the third character in the love plot. He is a beautiful youth with the face of a girl. He had visited the young widow once before, and she had fallen in love with him. One morning, "rosier than her name," she unexpectedly entered Théodore's bedroom "with nothing on her" but a transparent chemise, but to no avail. Théodore was unresponsive to her embraces and caresses. But Théodore's ambiguous charm and ambiguous

beauty now arouse D'Albert's desires. The unforeseen longing
for union with a man is a disturbing temptation. In this novel in
which sapphic unions feed the imagination of men no less than
women, *eros socraticus* is still taboo: "What a pity it is that he is a
man, or rather that I am not a woman." But perhaps D'Albert
need not accuse himself of an inclination that goes "against the
Order of Nature": "Théodore must be a woman disguised: . . .
Such beauty, even for a woman, is not the beauty of a man. . . .
It is a woman, by heaven, and I was very foolish to torment
myself in such a manner. In this way everything is explained in
the most natural fashion in the world, and I am not such a monster as I believed." "And I, poor monster," Viola/Cesario says
about herself. In idioms, going from Elizabethan times to the
nineteenth century, a "monster" (*le monstre*) was equated with a
homosexual.

In *Mademoiselle de Maupin* Gautier repeats the triangle of
Shakespearean eros. The Lady in Rose replaces the Dark Lady;
D'Albert, the first person of the narrative, replaces the first person of the *Sonnets*. At the base of this immutable triangle, the
new master mistress will take his place between the man and
the woman.

The gender of this accomplished horseman and "master of
the sword" with the face of a girl remains an enigma. In order
to solve the mystery of the infallibility of instinct and of the illusion of disguise, D'Albert decides to put on an amateur performance of *As You Like It* in the mansion of the Lady in Rose.
Rosette plays Phebe. Théodore plays Rosalind/Ganymede.

In the first scenes Rosalind is dressed as a woman. D'Albert
describes her first appearance: "There was a general cry of ad-
miration. The men applauded, and the women grew scarlet.
Rosette alone became extremely pale and leaned against the
wall, as though a sudden revelation were passing through her
brain. She made in a contrary direction the same movement as I
did. I always suspected her of loving Théodore." In the third

act Rosalind transformed into Ganymede is now dressed as a man: "Yet he was dressed in such a way," D'Albert continues, "as to give one a presentiment that these manly clothes had a feminine lining; a breadth of hip, a fulness of bosom, and a sort of undulation never seen in cloth on the body of a man, left but slight doubts respecting the person's sex. . . . My serenity returned to some extent, and I persuaded myself afresh that it was really a woman. I recovered sufficient composure to play my part in a fitting manner."

Rosalind from the production of *As You Like It* came to D'Albert during the night. She was a virgin. But the romantic Mademoiselle de Maupin had returned all the embraces, was "astonished at nothing," and was ready to prolong the pleasures unknown to her. When D'Albert woke up after "a soft, voluptuous sleep," Théodore/Rosalind was gone. He must have left at the break of day. The maid said that when she entered her mistress's room at noon as usual, the bed was disturbed and tossed and bore the impress of two bodies. When she made the bed she found two pearls similar to those Théodore wore in his hair when he played the part of Rosalind. The beautiful cavalier had not been seen by anyone. The following morning Théodore left, never to be heard or seen again by D'Albert or Rosette with whom he had divided that night.

Rosalind is Ganymede, and Ganymede is Rosalind. But what is Rosalind's gender? What is Ganymede's gender? In this startling reading, the new conclusion of *As You Like It* is bitter and free of illusions. From another time, from another novel— the novel was *Les Liaisons dangereuses*.

5

French literature written around the time of *Mademoiselle de Maupin* is astonishingly rich in works whose main and often sole theme is inversion, transvestitism, the double, castrato and hermaphrodite. Heroes of inversion have been known since the Renaissance, but outside that period and some masterpieces of the eighteenth century, such literature has been clandestine and pornographic. In the mid-1830s these figures appeared in works of the greatest writers of the period: Gautier, Musset, Mérimée, Balzac, and George Sand.

In a portrait by Delacroix painted in 1830, now at the Musée Carnavalet in Paris, George Sand is seen in a riding costume, a top hat—her dark hair streaming from underneath the broad brim—a high cravat, and a waistcoat with turned-down collar. At that time Sand preferred to wear men's attire.[15] Sand was then twenty-six years old. It was two years before her scandalous, almost open relationship with the beautiful Parisian actress Marie Dorval and a year before the publication of her novel *Lélia*.[16] Alfred de Musset, with whom Sand was about to have a romance, probably the most tempestuous in her entire life, in his letters always called her Lélia. In a letter to Sainte-Beuve Sand wrote: "I am utterly and completely Lélia. . . . I wanted to convince myself that that was not so."[17]

Lélia in the novel has a twin sister, Pulcheria, who can be taken for a mirror image of herself. When Lélia withdrew rather than confronting her first night of love, Pulcheria took her place in bed without being recognized. Although doubles physically, the two sisters have different souls. Lélia is frigid; Pulcheria is a courtesan in her constant need of a man. One of the earliest feminist manifestos, the novel shows that these are the two roles male morality reserves for woman. *Lélia* was considered scandalous in France almost until the advent of naturalism and in England for more than a century. Written by a woman, it disclosed woman's double eros. In youthful, sisterly incest, the two divided halves of the platonic apple are reunited for a brief moment, and Pulcheria experiences her first orgasm in the arms—covered with light down—of the sleeping Lélia.

But Lélia herself is split into two characters, a male and a female, and into two halves, one dark, the other fair (in George Sand's symbolism man is dark, woman is fair). From this juncture is born the Romantic androgyne of literature. "She has the ethereal features of a Tasso and the sad smile of a Dante. She has the boyish naturalness of Shakespeare's youthful heroines: she is Romeo, the poetic lover, Hamlet, the ascetic, pale visionary, and Juliet now half-dead, concealing the poison and the memory of her lover who broke her heart."[18]

Obsession with the theme of the androgyne—aesthetic, erotic, and social—seems to have been almost universal at that time. A year before *Lélia* and prior to starting his relationship with George Sand, Alfred de Musset wrote what is perhaps the best of all Romantic dramas, *Lorenzaccio*. The protagonist, a young Florentine prince at the time of the Renaissance, is even more internally divided than his literary prototype, Hamlet. He is also even more effeminate, a charge already made against Hamlet. Lorenzaccio's gender is shrouded in mystery to the very end. Undoubtedly he was intended as an androgyne. Perhaps for that reason, half a century had to elapse before the play could be put on the stage. It was first performed only in 1898 with Sarah Bernhardt in the title role. It proved to be one of her greatest triumphs: now sure of herself in the role of the androgyne, she decided to play Shakespeare's Hamlet.

Balzac's early novels are highly characteristic examples of the dark current of Romanticism. Not yet fully successful artistically, these works are nonetheless disturbing in their exploration of the sphere between the monstrous and bizarre that later fascinated Barbey d'Aurevilly and the surrealists, who called it *l'insolite*. In Balzac's *Seraphita*, where mysticism and physiology are strangely blended (as repeatedly happened thereafter), an androgyne, the angelic Seraphita, is adored by both a man, Wilfrid, and a young virgin girl, Minna.

Even more symptomatic is Balzac's *Girl with the Golden Eyes*, written in 1835, the year of *Mademoiselle de Maupin*'s publication. "A Sappho resurrected in Paris," writes an anonymous memoirist in *Souvenirs d'un demi-siècle*. "The passions of Sappho, who has been asleep for centuries on the rock of Leukos, have come back to life in Paris. Erynia, Mirra, Chloe, all those deserted nymphs, have reappeared in the penumbra of bedrooms like the restored frescoes of Greece."[19]

Paquita, the girl with the golden eyes, was brought from the southern isles and kept under strict guard in one of the great Parisian mansions. The marquise that brought Paquita to Paris, as Balzac writes in the preface to the first edition of the novel, "was a person brought up on islands where customs tolerate girls with golden eyes to such an extent that they have become almost an institution."[20]

From time to time Paquita could be sighted riding on the boulevards in a carriage with a black footman. De Marsay saw her one day, and the sight stirred his imagination. De Marsay reappears in later Balzac novels as a statesman and a minister, but in *The Girl with the Golden Eyes* he is still the most elegant of Parisian dandies. The description of De Marsay's morning toilet, with him seated in front of a mirror like a great actress preparing to go onstage, is one of the most brilliant scenes in the entire *Human Comedy*. De Marsay belonged to the secret Society of the Thirteen who, bound by inviolable oaths, put themselves above the law and did not recoil from murder and violence. "Through violence to pleasure," they would repeat as if they had learned it from the marquis de Sade himself.

De Marsay decided to win Paquita, and he won her by bribery and ingenuity. Paquita put the Argus guarding her to sleep with a dose of opium. She gave herself to De Marsay. Girls from faraway isles know all the secrets of love, and they are used to all forms of pleasure, but technically Paquita was a virgin. De Marsay wanted to be her first lover, but instead he was only her first man. That was not the innocence he had hoped to find in her body that smelled like a ripe peach. He felt deceived like Don Juan, who never found what he sought and was deceived by what he found.

De Marsay decided to punish in a bloody fashion the girl from Lesbos, but he was too late. In the boudoir covered with blood-red tapestry he found Paquita dying, her body mutilated and the marquise de San-Réal standing over her, dagger in hand. De Marsay caught her arm, and for a moment he and the marquise stood face to face. To their horror they saw in each other the same face, like the reflection in a mirror. The marquise, Paquita's true lover, and De Marsay, her one-night lover, were siblings, twin doubles. "In effect," Balzac concludes the story, "the two Menaechmi had not been more alike."

Balzac furnished an astonishing postscript to this bloody story. The author of the novel had met De Marsay when he was just barely seventeen. When he visited De Marsay ten years later, he could still discern a trace of "an extraordinary half-feminine beauty that so distinguished him as a boy." Thus in that lion of the Parisian salons Balzac detected a shade of the hermaphrodite.

The central character of Balzac's novel *Sarrasine* is a castrato. In eighteenth-century Rome under the name of Zambinella this operatic prima donna is a soprano and dancer famous for her beauty. Her voice and charms captivate the sculptor Sarrasine. He wants to sculpt her body. During their first physical contact, almost the moment before making love, though, Sarrasine discovers that the beautiful Zambinella is a disguised castrato. Like De Marsay who in Paquita's preserved virginity saw the "innocence" of a lesbian, Sarrasine exclaims: "Monster! For me, you have wiped women from the earth."[21] But for the author of *Mademoiselle de Maupin*, in the astonishing poem "Contralto" from the collection *Emaux et Camées*

(Enamels and Cameos), a castrato is the embodiment of "cursed beauty," a joining of a youth with a woman, Romeo with Juliet, like George Sand's Lélia. The castrato is a "monster," but in his multiple beauty he is a *monstre charmant*.

> Chimère ardente, effort suprême
> De l'art et de la volupté,
> Monstre charmant, comme je t'aime
> Avec ta multiple beauté![22]

In Balzac's *Sarrasine* a castrato in eighteenth-century Rome is an actress who arouses desire in men; in nineteenth-century Paris a nearly hundred-year-old man contracts a symbolic *mariage blanc* with the very young and disturbingly beautiful Mariannine, disturbingly beautiful because she is an exact copy of her twin brother. So even here the castrato is accompanied by a double. Man/woman, his/her, with him / with her are intermixed as though they were as mutually complementing/annihilating in *Sarrasine* as in Lodge's pastoral romance two and a half centuries earlier. In *Sarrasine* signs and meanings are interchangeable and fluid; grammar and anatomy have ceased to give unequivocal answers. It should not come as a surprise that in the past twenty years this novel has been the most frequently and extensively discussed text, challenging for structuralists and poststructuralists, for phenomenologists and post-Marxists, for deconstructionists and linguistic critics alike. Roland Barthes, who in his *S/Z*—the most hermetic of them all—has analyzed one by one all the 561 *lexias* of the novel, observes: "*Sarrasine* represents the very confusion . . . the unbridled (pandemic) circulation of signs, of sexes, of fortunes."[23]

The castrato, hermaphrodite, and double do not conform to systems of binary classification. Viola in *Twelfth Night* was called a eunuch. Freud in his late "pre-Lacanian" frenzies of intuition has shown the similarity of the threat—"the uncanny" (*das Unheimliche*)—of the double and the castrato.[24]

In his anthropological essays on differences and similarities among various cultures, Victor Turner writes that for the Ndembu and neighboring people in northwestern Zambia the number of children is the first sign of wealth and that the women are proud of their fertile wombs. But the birth of twins is greeted with horror, especially twins of the same gender. They do not belong to the existing system of kinship, where every member of the clan has a fixed place. Newborn twins are frequently killed, both or only one, but in that case which one? But *la pensée sauvage* has found a solution. In Zambia besides the system of classification there is always the shaman. Twins may be given to the shaman to be brought up as his successors. The village chief and his wives and offspring also remain outside the system of classification. Twin sisters are often removed shortly after birth to a separate hut belonging to the chieftain, located outside the clan's village.[25]

In binary oppositions woman is not-man. Man is not-woman. In the axiom of the excluded middle there is no place for the castrato. The castrato whose gender has been removed is a negation of the opposition between the sexes. The double is a negation of the opposition: I and not-I. I am the other, but the other is also me. Doubles, who as in Balzac's early novels are brother and sister, are a double hermaphrodite and hence again a negation of opposition. Such considerations may seem no more than playing with abstractions, but they reveal, although differently than in Freud, the same *threat* that the mere presence of the castrato, the hermaphrodite, and the clone calls forth. In the theater, especially in comedy, the disguise of gender has a long tradition and serves to amuse. But in the novel in the mid-1830s the sudden proliferation of the theme of disguised gender seems bewildering.

Mimicry on a broader scale is the counterpart of disguised gender in literary fiction. It is in Barthes's formulation the "pandemic" of signs and modes in onomastics, in manners, and in the social tissue itself. The most pronounced proliferation took place during the Restoration and after the events of 1830. During the French Revolution the basic patterns of time and space were violated for the first time. The calendar started with the first day of the French Republic, the months changed their names and their numbers of days, *citoyen* replaced *monsieur*, and streets and squares changed their patrons; for example, the Place Louis XIV became William Tell.

During the Restoration, as in our own experience, history was rewritten retroactively: neither the French Revolution nor the empire ever occurred. In the charter of 1814 Louis XVIII announced: "Given in Paris, in the year of grace 1814 and the eighteenth year of our reign." The son of Louis XVI, of course, never assumed the throne and consequently never became Louis XVII. Louis XVIII therefore assumed the throne in that fiction of legitimacy, following the death of "Louis XVII," who in this same newly rewritten history supposedly was crowned king two years to the day after his father Louis XVI was guillotined.

In 1830, still half a year before the July Revolution, "pandemic" broke loose first in the theater—at least in its pit seats. During every one of the forty performances of Hugo's *Hernani* the hooters and hissers and the applauders tried to drown out one another, leading to frequent fistfights. Gautier did not miss a single performance, always sporting his famous red vest. In the battle of *Hernani* the *perruques* and Romantics were hardly fighting over the place of a caesura in the classical alexandrine.

After 1830 the young Romantics became more frenetic. Gautier now belonged to the Petit Cénacle along with Petrus Borel and Nerval. Petrus, called The Lycanthrope, was already insane, and Nerval was but a step away from madness. Madness can be black or white. Petrus's madness was black, as was

Lautréamont's and Jarry's. In this opposition of colors, Nerval's insanity was white. Madness is always a disguise of reason, but when reason is mad, then madness is rational.

And 1830 once more. The subtitle of Stendhal's *Le Rouge et le noir* is *Chronique de 1830*. As a secretary for the marquis de la Mole, Julien Sorel always wore the black of a priest. When the marquis, confined to bed by the gout, invites him to his room, he has Julien put on a blue suit. In this costume he treats him as an equal. Dressed in black, Julien was just a little above a servant. Dressed in blue, this son of a peasant is *le chevalier* de la Vernaye and almost a relative of the marquis.

Even before disguised gender started to appear widely in novels, ancestral titles also became a disguise. In that merry-go-round of classes and fortunes, shopkeepers' daughters would exchange their dowries for aristocratic connections. The daughters of the nouveaux riches could not be distinguished from pauperized princesses and marquises. During Louis XVIII's reign the aristocracy became the bourgeoisie, disguised in its costumes.

In the postscript of 1830 to *Sarrasine*, Balzac wrote: "Contemporary society by leveling all class distinctions and throwing the same light on everything has destroyed the difference between the tragic and the comic." Binary systems of poetics have collapsed, just as has the binary opposition: aristocracy and bourgeoisie. Disguised class! Disguised gender!

Rosalind's gender. Exactly what is her gender? The gender of Rosalind seems to be dictated by history. Yet history on various levels and in various versions is present in everything contemporary, either openly or more often in disguised form. Striking evidence of this can be found in the differing interpretations of Shakespeare and in the stage history of his plays over the centuries. Contrary to the erroneous notions of many theater directors and scene designers, neither costumes nor settings are decisive in the never-ending tug-of-war between tradition and innovation, between the past and the present. The Forest of Arden in *As You Like It*, to which Rosalind flees disguised as Ganymede, can equally well be presented as the countryside near Stratford at the time of the Renaissance or as the byways of the Palais Royal in the Romantic Paris of Gautier and Balzac, the Bois de Boulogne of the Belle Epoque, or the Parc Monceau where young Proust and Gilberte played hopscotch. Gilberte had her hair in braids, or perhaps she wore a sailor suit. We might also recognize a far grimmer Forest of Arden in Berlin's Unter den Linden during the Third Reich or in the streets of Soho in New York today. Shakespeare's Rosalind on the contemporary stage is accompanied by the shadows of all the Rosalinds who have disguised themselves as Ganymede—and by all the myths, all the obsessions, all the temptations of androgynous eros, all the ebb and flow of the ever-recurring past.

Notes

1. Quotations of Shakespeare's plays are from the Arden Shakespeare editions: *Antony and Cleopatra*, ed. M. R. Ridley (London, 1962); *As You Like It*, ed. Agnes Latham (London, 1975); and *Twelfth Night*, ed. J. M. Lothian and T. W. Craik (London, 1975). The *Sonnets* are quoted from the edition edited by C. Knox Pooler (London, 1918).

2. Jean Genet, *The Blacks*, trans. B. Frechtman (New York, 1960), 3.

3. Northrop Frye, *A Natural Perspective: The Development of Shakespearean Comedy and Romance* (Cambridge, Mass., 1969), 123.

4. "A woman's part" implies pudendum, also penis and testicles. James T. Henke, *Courtesans and Cuckolds: A Glossary of Renaissance Dramatic Bawdy* (New York, 1979). It seems that in the subtext of eros the Duke describing Viola/Cesario oscillates between the anatomy of a girl and a boy.

5. *Perfect* (bot.): "Having all four whorls of the flower"; *Youth*: "novelty," "sexually curious," "amorous" (*O.E.D.*). "Perfect in lying down" means apt in lovemaking; Eric Partridge, *A Dictionary of Slang and Unconventional English* (New York, 1937). "Come, Kate, thou are perfect in lying down" (*Henry IV*, Part I, III.i.226); often in Shakespeare "a youth with its

sexual curiosity and amorous ardour." Provost on the pregnant Juliet: "a gentlewoman of mine, / Who falling in the flaws of her own youth" (*Measure for Measure*, see also *Merchant of Venice* V.iii.222). *Fancy*: a fancy woman, kept woman, "fancy man," or "fancy Joseph: harlot protector"; Partridge, *Dictionary*. "Fancy house: brothel"; Albert Barrère and Charles G. Leland, eds., *A Dictionary of Slang, Jargon and Cant*, (London, 1889–90; Detroit, 1967). "To take in a fancy work: to be addicted to the secret prostitution"; John S. Farmer and W. E. Henely, *Slang and Its Analogues* (1890–1904; New York, 1970), 2:374.

6. Shakespeare's choice of names is revealing. In Christian art from the late Middle Ages through the Renaissance until the late baroque, Sebastian and Adam were the only males allowed to be shown in the nude. With his girlish face and body almost resembling those of a young girl as seen in paintings by Guido Reni and Lorenzo Costa, Sebastian, clad only in a loincloth, pierced with arrows, whose smile in suffering seems close to ecstasy, has always been a favored sign for homosexuals. Antonio, too, seems to be a significant name: not without reason did Shakespeare so name his merchant of Venice, Bassanio's platonic friend ready for every sacrifice. Julia in *The Two Gentlemen of Verona* (in some respects a first version of *Twelfth Night*) chooses the name Sebastian when she disguises herself as a boy. Sebastian and Antonio appear to be signifying signs.

7. *Queene*: "a male homosexual, especially the effeminate partner in a homosexual relationship," from 1924 (*O.E.D.*). In the Renaissance, "effeminate mannere." The absence of slang notations from earlier periods does not necessarily mean they did not exist. In the sixteenth and seventeenth centuries *queen* was often denoted by the spelling "queene" or "quean." From the early Middle Ages (tenth century) a term of abuse, a hussy, a harlot, a strumpet (especially in the sixteenth and seventeenth centuries) (*O.E.D.*). In Shakespeare, an almost disparaging term: "A witch, a quean, an old cozening quean!" (*The Merry Wives of Windsor*), and, more vivid, "a scolding quean" (*All's Well That Ends Well*). In the seventeenth century: "All spent in a Tauerne amongst a consort of queanes and fiddlers" (Nashe, *Almond for Parrat*). The most interesting and chronologically close to Shakespeare: "A certain paultry Quean in mans apparel, that would pass for a Lady" (1670). A "quean's evil" is gonorrhea (*A Trick to Catch the Old One* V.ii.214). Henke, *Courtesans and Cuckolds*.

8. "Style is the weapon of these self-styled queens, their consorts and their entourages. Style is all-pervasive in speech, vocabulary, manner, dress and attitude. Style is a way of appearing to be 'real,' that is, a way of appear-

ing to be something that, it is often apparent, one isn't." Vincent Canby, review of *Paris Is Burning*, a film about New York's "drag queens," *New York Times*, 14 March 1991.

9. See Janice Paran, "The Amorous Girl-Boy: Sexual Ambiguity in Thomas Lodge's *Rosalynde*," *Essays* 1 (1981): 91–97.

10. Christopher Marlowe, *Hero and Leander*, 11. 83–84, 147–48. From *The Anchor Anthology of Sixteenth-Century Verse*, ed. Richard S. Sylvester (Gloucester, Mass., 1983).

11. Jean-Paul Sartre, preface to *The Maids*, by Jean Genet (New York, 1954), 23.

12. Marcel Proust, *Remembrance of Things Past*, trans. C. K. Scott Moncrieff and Terence Kilmartin (New York, 1982).

13. In England women first appeared on the stage in the Restoration period. The roles most coveted by young actresses were those of girls disguised as boys in Shakespeare's comedies, called breeches parts. For the first time it was possible for women to display their legs. That was one of the reasons for the popularity of Shakespeare's comedies. "To the Theatre and there saw *Argalus and Parthenia*; where a woman acted Parthenia and came afterward on the Stage in man's clothes, and had the best legs that ever I saw; and I was very well pleased with it." *The Diary of Samuel Pepys*, ed. Robert Latham and William Matthews (Berkeley, Calif., 1970), 203 (28 Oct. 1661).

14. Théophile Gautier, *Mademoiselle de Maupin*, trans. Burton Rascoe (New York, 1923). All quotations are translated from the French by Jadwiga Kosicka.

15. A line from Byron's *Don Juan*, written in 1823, "this modern Amazon and a quean of queans" (*O.E.D.*) seems to fit perfectly George Sand as seen in the portrait by Delacroix.

16. The beautiful Mademoiselle des Touches, known as Camille Maupin, appears in Balzac's *Lost Illusions*. She is a semifictional portrait of George Sand. In the novel Camille's lover is the actress Coralie: "Coralie joua dans la pièce de Camille Maupin et contribua beaucoup à ce succès de l'illustre hermaphrodite littéraire." Honoré de Balzac, *Illusions perdues*, Collection Classique Garnier (Paris, 1961), 461.

17. George Sand to Charles-Augustin Sainte-Beuve, 8 July 1833, cited in André Maurois, *Lélia; ou, La Vie de George Sand* (Paris, 1952).

18. George Sand, *Lélia*, trans. with an introduction by Maria Espinoza (Bloomington, Ind., 1978).

19. Quoted in Honoré de Balzac, *L'Histoire des Treize*, ed. P. G. Castex.

20. Honoré de Balzac, *The Girl with the Golden Eyes*, trans. Ellen Marriage (New York, 1950). All quotations are from this edition.

21. Honoré de Balzac, *Sarrasine*, in *S/Z*, by Roland Barthes, trans. Richard Miller (New York, 1974).

22. Théophile Gautier, "Contralto," in *Emaux et Camées* (Paris, 1822).

23. Barthes, *S/Z*, 216. See Barbara Johnson, *The Critical Difference* (Baltimore, 1980); Frederic Jameson, *The Political Unconscious* (Ithaca, N.Y., 1981); Sandy Petrey, *Realism and Revolution: Balzac, Stendhal, Zola, and the Performances of History* (Ithaca, N.Y., 1988). The final part of my essay is much indebted to Petrey's book, its analysis and quotations.

24. Sigmund Freud, *Essais de psychoanalyse appliquée* (Paris, 1933), quoted in Shoshana Felman, *La Folie et la chose littéraire* (Paris, 1978), 69.

25. See Victor Turner, *The Ritual Process* (Ithaca, N.Y., 1969), 44ff.

Translated by Jadwiga Kosicka

HEAD FOR MAIDENHEAD,
MAIDENHEAD FOR HEAD

The Structure of Exchange
in Measure for Measure

George Whetstone's play *The Historie of Promos and Cassandra,* published in 1578 and long forgotten, is acknowledged as the main dramatic source of Shakespeare's *Measure for Measure.* I wish to present the interrelation between the two plays, not from the perspective of philological influences but as a transformation of one and the same structural model. To uncover such a transformation is at the same time to make a literary and, more important, a theatrical interpretation.

"Devided into two Commicall Discourses," announces the title page of *Promos and Cassandra.*[1] This division into two parts is essential to the dramatic model. *Measure for Measure,* as has been said many times, also breaks down into two parts, despite or independently of the division into acts and scenes. The first part leads to a tragic resolution; the second part ends comically. The exact point where Shakespeare's play is split has been indicated: the turning point is at line 196 of act III, scene i, or the moment when the Duke, disguised as a Friar, suggests a substitute for Isabella.

The first part of *Promos and Cassandra* is called a "commicall" discourse. Yet, as later in *Measure for Measure*, the oppositions seem insoluble and do not at all promise a happy ending: "In the fyrste parte is showne, the unsufferable abuse, of a lewde Magistrate: The vertuous behaviours of a chaste Ladye: The uncontrowled leawdness of a favoured Curtisan. And the undeserved estimation of a pernicious Parasyte." The adjectival qualifiers seem particularly significant here: the judge's license is "unsufferable," debauchery "uncontrowled," estimation "undeserved." Chastity is "vertuous." Perhaps even too "vertuous," as will be shown later.

In Whetstone's play the judge takes advantage of innocence as the courtesan abuses the highest office. The office corrupts virtue, just as vice corrupts the office. Law is to sex as sex is to law. Corrupted law and corrupted sex are reciprocally destructive. In the Argument from *Promos and Cassandra* we already find the basic oppositions of *Measure for Measure*.

2

The elements of "tragedy," units of plot, or "bundles of relations," as they are called by Lévi-Strauss, are identical in the first parts of both plays.

1. The ruler (King of Hungary in *Promos and Cassandra,* Duke of Vienna in *Measure for Measure*) goes abroad and leaves a substitute to rule in his place (Promos and Angelo, respectively).

2. The Deputy brings an old law against immorality back into practice.

3. A young lover (Andrugio in Whetstone, Claudio in Shakespeare) is sentenced to be beheaded.

4. The sister (Cassandra in Whetstone, Isabella in Shakespeare) pleads with the Deputy for mercy for her brother.

5. The Deputy demands her virginity in exchange for her brother's life.

6. The brother asks the sister to comply with the deal and save his head.

We can apply Lévi-Strauss's method of interpreting the Oedipus myths to present a graphic model of Whetstone and Shakespeare's plays. The plot units can be arranged in three vertical columns, Law, Sex, and Family Relations, in which the same oppositions of deficiency and excess, of below-the-measure and above-the-measure, between the underrated and the overrated, are repeated. This is diagrammatically represented in the accompanying table.

The opposition between oversatiation and lack of satisfaction, excess and scarcity, is already present in the first dialogue of Lucio and Claudio:

> LUCIO: Whence comes this restraint?
> CLAUDIO: From too much liberty, my Lucio. Liberty,
>   As surfeit, is the father of much fast;
>   So every scope by the immoderate use
>   Turns to restraint.
>
> (I.ii.116–20)[2]

The courtesan Lamia with her helpers in Whetstone and the bawds in *Measure for Measure* represent promiscuity beyond measure. Virginity is a sexual fast: sexual abstinence is below-the-measure. But Shakespearean Isabella is not only a virgin like Cassandra in Whetstone: she is also a novice, ready to take her religious vows. Celibacy is the underrating of family obligations. A brother who demands that his sister pay with her virginity for his head is overrating family duties. All

LAW		SEX		FAMILY	
Deficiency Underrated	**Excess Overrated**	**Deficiency Underrated**	**Excess Overrated**	**Deficiency Underrated**	**Excess Overrated**
The kingdoms of Hungary and Vienna before the ruler's departure	The Deputy	Chastity of Cassandra–Isabella	Premarital sex: Polina and Andrugio, Juliet and Claudio	"A sisterhood" (II.ii.21)	Brother demands of his sister that she sacrifice her virginity to save his life
"Too much liberty" (I.i.117)	"Our terror" (I.i.19)	"Fasting maids" (II.ii.158)	Pregnant Juliet	Isabella–the nun	"Incest" (III.i.138)
"Mercy" (I.i.44)	"Mortality" (I.i.44)	"Restraint" (I.ii.116)	"The immoderate use"	"More than our brother is our chastity" (II.iv.184)	"Might there not be a charity in sin, to save this brother's life" (II.iv.63)
Exchange of heads by the Provost: "make a scarecrow of the law" (II.i.1)	Beheading as punishment for unconsecrated cohabitation: Andrugio and Claudio are condemned to death, "heading and hanging" (II.i.234)	Angelo: "a man of stricture and firm abstinence" (I.iii.12)	Mistress Overdone; brothels and syphilis in Vienna		

oppositions become very sharp in Shakespeare. Sacrificing virginity to save the brother's head is compared to an incestuous relation, which for Lévi-Strauss is the highest degree of overrating family ties: "Is't not a kind of incest, to take life / From thine own sister's shame?" (III.i.138–39).

Juliet from *Measure for Measure* not only has a lover, but she is also pregnant ("The stealth of our most mutual entertainment / With character too gross is writ on Juliet," I.ii.157–58). Many detailed studies have been devoted to the differences and similarities between the premarriage contracts of Claudio and Juliet, and Angelo and Marianna. But in the dramatic perspective of *Measure for Measure* the oppositions are drawn clearly and distinctly. Excess of desire and too few legal bonds unite the pair of young lovers. Too many legal bonds without sexual desire connect Angelo and Marianna.

In *Measure for Measure* there are four female parts. The parallels and oppositions here appear essential and intentional. The procuress is called Mistress Overdone; Isabella might be called Miss Underdone in the first scene in the nunnery. But this Miss Underdone is a "maximalist" from the beginning. During her novitiate she complains of insufficient discipline:

> I speak not as desiring more
> But rather wishing a more strict restraint
> Upon the sisters stood, the votarists of Saint Clare.
> (I.iv.3–5)

The Shakespearean system of doubles in which, as in mirror, the left is right and the right is left, is particularly expressive in *Measure for Measure*. Isabella, a virgin and a would-be nun, has rosy cheeks like Briseis, Achilles' captive in the *Iliad,* who made his bedding every night in the tent. But the pregnant Juliet is "pale." The virgin-nun and the mistress are counterposed and at the same time related in Shakespeare:

ISABELLA: My cousin Juliet?
LUCIO: Is she your cousin?
ISABELLA: Adoptedly, as schoolmaids change their names.
By vain though apt affection.

(I.iv.44–47)

Cassandra from Whetstone's play is split in two in *Measure for Measure*; she is divided between Isabella and her substitute, Marianna. Marianna is a surrogate, the ritual sacrificial lamb: but in Shakespeare's ironic structure this lamb hurries willingly to be slaughtered.

3

Beheading is the punishment for deflowering a virgin without a proper marriage. The old law reinstated in the Hungarian kingdom and in Vienna is the measure-for-measure law. But the ransom is another exchange. For her brother's head, the sister is to pay with her maidenhead: head for maidenhead, and maidenhead for head.

The Deputy does not keep his word and demands that the head be sent to him after all. Only a substitute head can save the brother's life. In this system of trading sex and law, everything is paid for in "heads." The "cutting off" of heads has very clear sexual connotations.

SAMPSON: I will be cruel with the maids; I will cut off
their heads.
GREGORY: The heads of the maids?
SAMPSON: Ay, the heads of the maids, or their maiden-
heads: take it in what sense you wilt.
(*Romeo and Juliet* I.i.23–26)

In *Measure for Measure* the dramatic exchange of heads corresponds to the system of linguistic transactions, in which an exchange of idiomatic meanings of *head* takes place. Pompey says: "Does your worship mean to geld and splay all the youth of the city? . . . If you head and hang all that offend that way but for ten year together, you'll be glad to give out a commission for more heads" (II.i.227–28, 235–37). Later he says, in his conversation with the Provost:

> PROVOST: Can you cut off a man's head?
> POMPEY: If the man be a bachelor, sir, I can; but if he be a married man he's his wife's head; and I can never cut off a woman's head.
>
> (IV.ii.1–4)

In both plays the head of an unhappy lover is exchanged for both the head of another prisoner and the maidenhead. "Not only must another head be found for Claudio," succinctly writes J. W. Lever in the introduction to the Arden edition, "but another maidenhead for Isabella's" (xlii). But Shakespeare is more cruel and cynical than Whetstone. Head for maidenhead, maidenhead for head, and still another head for head and maidenhead for maidenhead. In *Measure for Measure* we have a substitute maidenhead and not one but two substitute heads: "death's a great disguiser" (IV.ii.174).

In Whetstone it is the anonymous head of a "felon's newly executed." In Shakespeare the first substitute head is still very firmly attached to Barnardine's neck when the Duke blithely decides to send him to the next world. Barnardine is saved because he is in a drunken stupor.

> A creature unprepar'd, unmeet for death:
> And to transport him in the mind he is
> Were damnable.
>
> (IV.iii.66–68)

The condemned must be in the best of health and in full posses-
sion of his faculties in order for the execution to take place: this
is a very long-standing Christian tradition, from Shakespeare's
time until ours. But a new head has just been found: Ragozine,
"a most notorious pirate," died just in time "of a cruel fever"
while in prison.

In *Measure for Measure* one can distinguish yet a third "topo-
graphical" structure, that of places of action, in which the oppositions correspond to the structure of exchange on the plot
and lexical levels. There are six distinct places of action: the
Duke's palace, the streets of Vienna, Saint Clare's nunnery, the
monks' monastery, Marianna's moated grange, and the prison.

In the Duke's palace, where the Deputy had been installed,
the law orders heads to fall. In the streets of Vienna where Mistress Overdone and the bawd Pompey conduct their trade,
"heads" are also cut off. "Immoderate use" corrupts both nature and nurture in Vienna. In this imaginary landscape the palace and the street represent the fundamental opposition of law
and sex in excess. The monastery and the nunnery, Marianna's
house and the prison, are the places of consecutive exchanges.
The cloister is no shelter from sex and is not above the power
of law. Isabella, a novice nun, is made a shameless offer of her
brother's life for her virginity.

As soon as she begins her novitiate, she has already learned
the road from "restraint" to "immoderate use" and is shuttling
between the palace and the prison night and day. In the monastery the Duke disguises himself as a Friar and toys with the
condemned like a cat with a mouse, preparing him for the fake
execution ("be absolute for death," III.i.6) with a cruel sadistic
test. He takes advantage of the secret of confession for his own
ends and finds a substitute bedmate and a substitute maidenhead for his own substitute, the Deputy: "Here comes a man,
of comfort, whose advice / Hath often still'd my brawling dis-
content" (IV.i.8–9). The "man of comfort" will substitute

Marianna for Isabella in Angelo's bed. In the garden in front of Marianna's grange, an exchange of maidenheads is arranged; in prison, real heads are exchanged.

There are two other significant places in *Measure for Measure* where the action takes place offstage: the "grange" of Mistress Overdone and Angelo's "garden house." *House* has many different connotations in the play: "hot-house," "ill-house," "bawd-house," "naughty-house," "tap-house," "house of profession," "houses of resort." Twenty times during the play *house* signifies brothel, and perhaps it is not accidental that Angelo's palace is twice called a "garden house" (V.i.211, 228; IV.i.28).

Shakespeare's cruel vision is infallible: the prison, always and everywhere, is a crossroads where corrupted rulers meet corrupted sex. The bawd Pompey meets all his old friends here: "I am as well acquainted here as I was in our house of profession; one would think it were Mistress Overdone's own house, for here be many of her old customers" (IV.ii.1–4). But Pompey was brought from the brothel to the prison in order to be the executioner's helper: "I have been an unlawful bawd time out of mind, but yet I will be content to be a lawful hangman" (IV.ii.14–16).

The executioner and the bawd are always on close terms with the establishment. They both represent law and sex beyond measure. In seventeenth-century English, where *dying* has its second, sexual connotation, the executioner and the bawd equally help in "dying." The victims of procurer and of executioner have the same bodies. As Stanislaw Jerzy Lec wrote in his cruel aphorism: "Their bodies were so close together that there was no room for real affection."[3] The procurer and the bawd think in the same way.

In order to cut off a head one needs an executioner and his helper. The bawd, a "helper" in sex, standing beyond the law, becomes the executioner's assistant and the executioner of the law. Now the bawd's post is vacant, but for too short a time. In order to bring another virgin to Angelo in place of Isabella, a new bawd and a new executioner are needed.

> ISABELLA: Show me how, good father.
> DUKE: . . . We shall advise this wronged maid to stead up your appointment. . . . by this, is your brother saved, your honour untainted, the poor Marianna advantaged. . . . The maid will I frame, and make fit for his attempt.
>
> (III.i.238ff.)

In this scene the Duke speaks like a professional: "the maid will I frame," he says and, a few lines later, "gives him promise of satisfaction." The first procurer in the play is Pompey, transformed into the executioner's helper. The second procurer is the Duke himself disguised as a Friar. But without Isabella's help the "bed trick" cannot be accomplished.

Isabella, the subtle sophist, bargaining with bodies and souls (in the nunnery she might have had time to pore over theological treatises on sexual morality), saves her *own* soul ("I had rather give my body than my soul," II.iv.56) but gives the other's body to Angelo. Angelo coldly calls this "vice" which Catholic Isabella so much abhors "sweet uncleanliness" (II.iv.54). Mistress Overdone had been named Madam Mitigation, and now in turn the nun with "cheek-roses" (I.iv.16) becomes the new dispenser of this "sweet uncleanliness."

When her brother desperately begs her to save his life at the cost of her chastity, Isabella replies with disgust:

> O fie, fie, fie!
> Thy sin's not accidental, but a trade;
> Mercy to thee would prove itself a bawd.
> (III.i.147–49)

Yet in the same scene, barely having recovered from her indignation, she agrees without hesitation to procure for Angelo and substitute poor Marianna in her own place. "I thank you for this comfort," says Isabella before her exit.

The Constable now enters, joined by the bawd Pompey and the officers. The entire third act takes place in prison. The action proceeds at the fast pace of Stuart theater, and the first words of Elbow, the Constable, are juxtaposed with Isabella's words: "Nay if there be no remedy for it, but that you will needs buy and sell men and women like beasts, we shall have all the world drink brown and white bastard" (III.ii.1–4).

Act III ends the tragic development of *Measure for Measure,* and the plot begins to turn toward the "comic" resolution. The price for this "happy" ending is the exchange of maidenheads. The simple Constable offers a realistic evaluation of this "happy bargain": there is "no remedy" for this world. The Duke "of dark corners," disguised as a "ghostly father," can only exclaim after the Constable: "O heavens, what stuff is here" (III.ii.5).

4

The timing in Shakespeare's theater is often vague or ambiguous. But when a precise hour of day or night is given it always has special dramatic value: "But he must die tomorrow" (IV.ii.91). In *Measure for Measure* "tomorrow" is mentioned twenty-six times, and fourteen of these menacing "tomorrows" refer to Claudio's impending death. In this dramatic "tomorrow," the hour of execution is constantly approaching, until at last Angelo orders the execution for precisely four o'clock in the morning.

"Tomorrow" Isabella is to speak with Angelo. And this "tomorrow," uttered seven times, rapidly shrinks and becomes the hour, late at night or early in the morning, when Marianna is to go to Angelo's garden house. This very same late night or early morning hour Juliet's labor begins: "What shall be done, sir, with the groaning Juliet? / She's very near her hour" (II.ii.15–16).

In this sudden condensation of Shakespearean time, the hours of night and day are given with increasing precision. " 'Tis now dead midnight" (IV.ii.63): the idiom *dead* is suddenly revalued as the hour of death approaches. And a few lines further on: "Good morrow; for, as I take it, it is almost day" (IV.ii.103). At the end of the scene, "it is almost clear dawn" (IV.ii.209).

At the same hour of late night and early morning (even the day of the week is given: "But Tuesday night once gone," V.i.228), Marianna is losing her virginity in Isabella's place. Juliet is about to give birth, and her lover is about to lose his head. In the mythical order the mediation between life and death is the sexual act of conception. In Shakespeare's synchrony the hour of birth, the hour of death, and the hour at which lovers unite is the same hour. But in *Measure for Measure* only Juliet's labor is real. In place of Claudio's real head a false head of a prisoner who is already dead is substituted. Instead of Isabella, Marianna lies with Angelo. In both exchanges the head and the maidenhead are counterfeit. Four o'clock that Wednesday morning the tragedy of *Measure for Measure* turns into its opposite.

On the tragic plane, the sister sacrifices her honor for her brother, the Deputy does not keep his promises, the brother is executed, and the dishonored sister takes her own life.

> Is there no remedy?
> None, but such remedy as, to save a head,
> To cleave a heart in twain.
>
> (III.i.60–63)

The rightful ruler would in turn condemn the traitor to death. Justice would be reestablished, but at the cost of at least three corpses onstage in the epilogue of a tragedy.

In this unrealized tragic plan which has its roots in the first part of the play, sex and death are connected in a constant, intruding, and nearly obsessive idiom of "dying" in the sexual act and in the act of execution: "And strip myself to death as to bed" (II.iv.102). The executioner's name, Abhorson, unites in itself "abhor" and "whore-son."[4] For Isabella sex is a "pollution," and she compares the "horror" of defloration to blood spilt during an execution. This virgin with rosy cheeks has a sadomasochistic imagination indeed; as in the contemporary catechism for young ladies, sex is linked in her imagination with all the tortures of hell. Even if her brother had twenty heads, says Isabella, it would be better to deposit them on twenty blocks than to have his sister yield her body to "such abhorr'd pollution" (II.iv.182). "If I must die," says Claudio, "I will encounter darkness as a bride / And hug it in mine arms" (III.i.82–84). For unhappy Juliet "the injurious law"[5] is a "dying horror" (III.ii.40–41).

Sex and law are violence and rape. Eros and death are connected with each other in a dramatic and linguistic intertwining within the recurring exchange of one measure for another: "Like rats that ravin down their proper bane, / A thirsty evil; and when we drink, we die" (I.ii.121–22).

5

In *Measure for Measure* the change of resolution from tragic to comic is effected through a series of exchanges and substitutes whose manipulator, like a puppeteer pulling his marionette's strings, is the Duke disguised as a Friar. In *Promos and Cassandra* the transition from the tragic to the comic ending is the return

of the absent king, who, like the Lord's anointed, punishes sin-
ners and rewards the virtuous. In Shakespeare, the "happy"
ending results from a system of *transaction,* in Whetstone
through *mediation.* Both plays are broken down into "tragic" and "comic"
parts. But the break occurs at different points in the plot. In
Shakespeare it is when a substitute for Isabella is found, in
Whetstone at the King's dispensation of mercy. "In the second
parte is discursed the perfect magnanimitye of a noble kinge, in
checking Vice and favouringe Vertue: wherein is showne, the
Ruyne and overthrowe, of dishonest practises: with the ad-
vancement of upright dealing."

Marriage is a mediation between the excess of sex and the
absence of law. Between the merciless law which demands the
death of the culprit and the scarcity of justice the mediation is
constituted by the mercy of the Lord's anointed. Angelo is
condemned to marry Marianna just as Promos is forced hur-
riedly to marry Cassandra. Angelo, like Promos, is then to lose
his head on the block and, like Promos, is saved thanks to the
wife he married *in extremis.* In both plays the Deputy leaves un-
harmed. But the meaning of the marriage and of mercy is not
the same in both plays.

Cassandra gives up her honor to save her brother. The Roman *virtus* was not the virtue of virginity, but heroic self-
sacrifice. Cassandra's sacrifice is a heroic choice: "The Kinge, to
knowe the vertues of Cassandra, pardoned both him [An-
drugio] and Promos." Marianna's marriage and the Duke's pardon for Angelo are not the same as a restitution for lost honor
and a reward for virtue, but constitute both a sanctioning of
blackmail and a trap:

> Craft against vice I must apply.
> With Angelo tonight shall lie
> His old betrothed, but despised:

> So disguise shall by th' disguised
> Pay with falsehood false exacting,
> And perform an old contracting.
>
> (III.ii.270–75)

The premarriage contract that Angelo has made with Marianna is fulfilled in bad faith by both parties. The blackmailer is in turn blackmailed ("pay with falsehood false exacting"), as in an old farce where a cheat is cheated. Both sides are of equal worth. The Duke does not seem to have any doubts about this: "Well, Angelo, your evil quits you well. Look that you love your wife: her worth, worth yours." Angelo's release is not a Christian act of mercy, but a measure for measure.[6] Otherwise the title of this comedy of errors would not make any sense.

But in the epilogue of *Measure for Measure* there is yet another forced marriage. Lucio, a "fantastic," plays a role similar to that of a Shakespearean fool. He belongs to "good society" but is outside it at the same time. He also belongs to "bad company," although he remains outside it as well. He is the only figure in the play who constantly commutes between the ducal palace, the prison, and the brothels in Vienna. He is also the only disinterested character, free of illusions as well as of prejudices. He sees clearly what is going on around him. He even makes a fool of the ruler. But unlike the other fools in Shakespeare, Lucio is only a self-proclaimed jester. He plays the fool but does not wear a motley's costume. In his "sorry fooling" he dares to criticize the rulers. For this he can't go scot-free.

Only Lucio, of all the characters, is punished at the end.[7] Even Barnardine, "a dissolute prisoner," is released from his cell. In the "happy" end, the Duke kindly allows Lucio to choose between a flogging and hanging, or marrying a whore. For Lucio there is not much difference between these choices:

> LUCIO: Marrying a punk, my Lord, is pressing to death,
> whipping, and hanging.
> DUKE: Slandering a prince deserves it.
>
> (V.i.520–22)

Lucio's last lines toward the end of the play seem to be, as often in Shakespeare, a collective formula of the play's themes or its antimoral. In *Promos and Cassandra* the procurers and whores are expelled from the Hungarian kingdom to which justice and virtue are returning together with the King. In this last exchange of *Measure for Measure* the marriage to a "punk" is substituted for a hangman's rope. A whore or the rope, the rope or the whore remain as the sole alternatives for Shakespearean Vienna. Corrupted law or corrupted sex.

The staging of the epilogue is most important in the theatrical interpretation of *Measure for Measure*. In the traditional performances the wedding pageant of three couples ends the play. In the 1955 BBC production, *Measure for Measure* was interpreted, according to the prevailing Christian reading, as a parable of mercy and divine atonement, and the wedding pageant was accompanied by the ringing of the bells as for Resurrection and a Magnificat.[8]

The first couple leading the pageant is the Duke and Isabella. But the Duke, taking Isabella for his wife, does not even ask her consent. She is the only young maid whose virginity is preserved until the end of the play. This maidenhead is the last price for the "happy ending" and the wedding present for the supreme judge. Marianna and Angelo, forced to marry by the Duke, form the second couple. The third couple in this merry pageant is the recently pardoned Claudio and Julia, who the night before had been released from prison so that she could give birth in peace. If one is to read into the text what is implied by it, Julia should walk in the wedding pageant with an infant at her breast or, at least, "very near her hour," move very slowly in the last hours before the delivery.

Then there is Lucio. In this pageant Lucio and the Provost are the last "wedding couple." The play's editors often add an exit for Lucio before the Duke's last speech so that his presence in chains will not destroy the festive mood. But the last scene of *Measure for Measure,* in a "public place near the city gate," appears to be a repetition of the second scene of act I, also in a public place in Vienna. Instead of Claudio's being led in chains, now the Provost is leading the enchained Lucio.

In the latest productions of *Measure for Measure* in Stratford, Ontario, in Birmingham, and in Giessen, Isabella's silence in response to the Duke's proposal took on a particular meaning. In the Canadian production, Isabella was left alone in the epilogue; frightened and astounded, she tore the nun's cornet from her head.[9] In Giessen she was also left alone on the stage, in a white dress and a veil, dressed for the marriage as though for the coffin. But the most consistent solution of the "happy ending" in *Measure for Measure* would be to leave Isabella together with enchained Lucio alone on the stage.

In *Measure for Measure* the Duke and the Deputy "together" marry Cassandra from Whetstone's play; Cassandra is split between Isabella and her substitute. In the theatrical tradition Isabella is usually counterposed to Marianna as strongly as the Duke is to the Deputy. But in *Measure for Measure* the structure of exchange, substitutes, and doubles also constitutes a theatrical score. Not only is Cassandra split into Isabella and Marianna, but the ruler is also split between his surrogate, the Deputy Angelo, and the ruler, himself disguised as a Friar, split between manifest and hidden rule, between the secular and the clerical:

> I have on Angelo impos'd the office;
> Who may in th' ambush of my name strike home,
> And yet my nature never in the fight
> To do in slander. And to behold his sway,
> I will, as 'twere a brother of your order,
> Visit both prince and people.
>
> (I.iii.40–45)

The ruler is split between the supreme judge and the manipulator, the apparatus and the big ear, which eavesdrops not only on his subjects but on the surrogate ruler himself: "I am confessor to Angelo, and I know this to be true" (III.i.165). Angelo is compared to a coin with heads and tails. But these two sides, mercy and mortality, are the ruler himself. The ruler is a judge and a confessor who sends prisoners off to death and who falsely absolves them from sin in the last hour. The ruler is a law against rape and a rape of the law, and the law which rapes:

> A deflower'd maid;
> And by an eminent body, that enforc'd
> The law against it!
>
> (IV.iv.19–21)

In this new *Prince* of Machiavelli, the Duke in his two disguises is the merciless avenging god of the Puritans and the Catholic god of capricious mercy. But both gods punish a critique of the rulers.

In a production which attempted to convey the "score" of the play, its repetitions and transformations, Isabella and Marianna, the Duke and the Deputy, should correspond to each other like a figure and its reflection in a mirror. The structure of exchange in *Measure for Measure,* in which the right is left and the left is right, is at the same time its aesthetics and its ideology.

Whetstone's *Promos and Cassandra* is a bizarre mixture of a Renaissance novella with a belated medieval morality play. When the Lord's anointed leaves, evil triumphs over the good; when the Lord's anointed returns, virtue triumphs over vice, and the evil is vindicated and banned. Through a variation on the same model, the morality play is translated into an antimorality play, in which the angels bubble over with laughter when they observe men's apish gambols from their heavenly heights:

> But man, proud man,
> Dress'd in a little brief authority
> . . . like an angry ape
> Plays such fantastic tricks before high heaven
> As makes the angels weep; who, with our spleens,
> Would all themselves laugh mortal.
>
> (II.ii.118–23)

Notes

1. All quotations from Whetstone are from the 1578 edition of *Promos and Cassandra*.

2. All quotes from *Measure for Measure* are from the Arden Shakespeare edition, ed. J. W. Lever (New York, 1965). The quotation from *Romeo and Juliet* is from the New Shakespeare edition, ed. John Dover Wilson and G. I. Duthie (Cambridge, 1959).

3. Stanisław Jerzy Lec. *Unkempt Thoughts,* trans. Jacek Galazka (New York, 1962), 73.

4. See Lever, ed., *Measure for Measure,* introduction, note to IV.ii.18.

5. I adopt Hammer's emendation: "law," rather than "love."

6. Johnson's comment is worth noting: "Angelo's crimes were such as must sufficiently justify punishment, whether its end be to secure the innocent from wrong or to deter guilt by example; and I believe every reader feels

some indignation when he finds him spared. From what extenuation of his crime can Isabel, who yet supposes her brother dead, form any plea in his favour. *Since he was good, till he looked on me, let him not die.* I am not afraid our varlet poet intended to incalculate that women think ill of nothing that raises the credit of their beauty and are ready, however virtuous, to pardon any act which they think incited by their own charms." Quoted from *Samuel Johnson on Shakespeare,* ed. W. K. Wimsatt, Jr. (New York, 1960), 76.

7. The reading by Johnson is, as usual, full of good sense: "After the pardon of two murderers, Lucio might be treated by the good duke with less harshness; but perhaps the poet intended to show, what is too often seen, *that men easily forgive wrongs which are not committed against themselves.*" Ibid.

8. Directed by Nevill Coghill and Raymond Raikes. See Lever, ed., *Measure for Measure,* p. lvii.

9. Directed by Robin Philips. See Alexander Leggatt, "The Extra Dimension: Shakespeare in Performance," *Mosaic* 10, no. 3 (1977): 46–47.

Translated by Mark Rosenzweig

THE GUILLOTINE AS A
TRAGIC HERO

Julius Caesar *and Büchner's*
Danton's Death

Danton: The truth, the bitter truth.
—Stendhal, *The Red and the Black*

T ragedy is the severing of a human destiny. In this severing the beginning and the end acquire a special significance. Historical tragedy is the severing of a historical sequence. In this severing the beginning and the end are even more meaningful. Inherent in them is not only a dramatic condensation of time but also the hero's choice of tragic history. Not only can its protagonists be tragic, but history itself can also become a tragic hero.

In the late English Middle Ages (1485), a tragedy was called a chapter. Now a chapter has its beginning, its end, and its length. A life was the measure of a chapter; it was its beginning and its end. The lives of saints in the history of religion, of famous statesmen in the republics of antiquity, and of rulers of kingdoms seem to constitute "natural" chapters. This tradition goes back, of course, to Plutarch. For Plutarch, history was the story of Greece and Rome. Its chapters are *vitae,* and in Plutarch they are arranged in parallel lives. Greek history repeats itself in Roman history in characters of its famous statesmen. What changes are the names of the leaders and the names of the massacred towns and the conquered provinces, but what remains constant for Plutarch is the common pantheon of Greece and Rome. For that reason Julius Caesar could be compared with Alexander the Great.

The composition of history in parallel lives, made classic for many centuries by Plutarch, was dethroned and replaced by another principle of analogy by Giovanni Boccaccio in his *De casibus virorum illustrium* (1373). Worthy of particular note in these new chapters about the fall of princes is the use of the plural. In this perception of history at the threshold of the Italian Renaissance, the lives of princes, in contradistinction to Plutarch, are similar in Boccaccio's view not in *virtu,* not even in cruelty, nor in triumphs or laurels, but solely in their inevitable downfall. Boccaccio knew the tragedies of both Euripides and Seneca, but he never called his chapters about the fall of princes tragedies. He probably did not know Aristotle, but what is striking is that his lives are "tragic" in the Aristotelian sense of the word. The most elemental example of tragedy in Aristotle's *Poetics* is the fall of a great man. This most telling image of tragic destiny—and also the most frequently encountered in common experience—reappeared in the definitions of tragedy found in Chaucer, as well as long before him and long after him. Tragedy is the fall from good fortune to bad fortune; the higher the rung, the more telling and exemplary the fall. The most exemplary of all is the fall of a king.

In the English Middle Ages, and perhaps not only the English, this model of tragedy was linked to the image of the changeable Wheel of Fortune, which was likewise taken from antiquity. In the *Holkham Bible,* which is one of the most beautiful illuminated English manuscripts and dates to the beginning of the fourteenth century, Fortune turns this huge royal merry-go-round. It raises up a young man with flowing hair and a crown in his hand. Then it places him on a throne at the top of this same merry-go-round with the crown on his head and a scepter in his hand. Next it hurls him down as a bearded old man with the crown falling off his head. Finally beneath the Wheel of Fortune the man is seen lying prone, stripped of his royal robes, without crown and scepter, half-naked and bare-footed. This regal tragedy consists of four acts: *Regnabo, Regno, Regnavi, Sum sine regna.* But perhaps what is most characteristic is the fact that in this medieval Bible the Grand Mechanism of royal history was placed at the very beginnings of the history of the Christian world and was, as it were, metaphysically sanctioned. On the leaf preceding the image of the Wheel of Fortune, there is a representation of the creation of the world with God the Father holding an enormous compass in his hand. On the same page is depicted Lucifer and the proud angels being cast into the abyss, similar to the fall of the king. Perhaps in this medieval Bible for the first time ever a historical tragedy becomes the tragedy of the world.

In *The Duchess of Malfi* Webster follows in the footsteps of the late medieval tragedy about Alexander: "When fortune's wheel is overcharged with Princes / The weight makes it move swift."[1] In times of terror the guillotine moves even more swiftly.

2

Shakespeare's *Julius Caesar* is perhaps the most famous and certainly one of the most moving examples of historical tragedies of a man's fall. Caesar is murdered at the height of his triumphs. A moment before his murder, almost in the last words of his final speech, he compared himself to the northern star "of whose true-fix'd and resting quality / There is no fellow in the firmament" (III.i.61–62).[2] Now he is lying bleeding on the steps of the Capitol pierced by the daggers of the Roman senators. Shakespeare saw with the utmost clarity that Caesar's death is a twofold exemplum of both history and tragedy and that it would be played all over again on the steps of many capitols and on the stages of many theaters: it would "be acted o'er, / In states unborn and accents yet unknown!" (III.i.112–13).

For Brecht that last deadly blow given Caesar by Brutus might well be an example of a *gestus* in which history for a split second becomes immobile, the way a single frame of a film is held on the screen, so that its sense could become transparent and engraved in our memory. There are two tragic actors in this scene of death on the Capitol steps at high noon: Caesar and Brutus. The tragedy is called *Julius Caesar,* but the first tragic actor dies in the middle of act III, almost exactly halfway through the drama. In political and rhetorical treatises and parallels beginning in the Middle Ages and continuing through the entire Renaissance until after the English and French revolutions, Brutus is alternately portrayed as a regicide and a tyrannicide. For the audacious deed of raising his hand against God's chosen, in Dante's *Divine Comedy* he is cast to the very bottom of hell next to Judas. Elsewhere he becomes the defender of liberty, the patron saint of terror for all times.

If the tragedy had ended in act III with the murder of Caesar and the funeral ceremonies, Caesar would have been its sole protagonist. Had it ended in act V with Brutus's suicide by running on his own sword, he would have been the secondary and perhaps even the primary protagonist, and the tragedy could have been called *Brutus.* But in the drama of history, besides Caesar and Brutus there are other principal actors: Cassius, a fanatical hater, a bribe giver and taker, who knows only too well that the end justifies the means and who alone could have saved the republic. But what kind of republic? There is also Mark Antony, a Renaissance type of politician with many faces who always sides with the Caesars, a rhetorician, a tacti cian, and a pragmatist. Finally, the most enigmatic character in the play, the one who always appears at the end, is Octavius, Julius's successor, the new Caesar, but a Caesar without a face. The meaning of a tragedy lies in the severing of its historical sequence, in the choice of its beginning and its end. In the first scene two tribunes try in vain to persuade the Roman tradesmen, who have spilled out onto the streets leading to the Capitol in order to celebrate Caesar's triumph, that they should go back to work. Not so long ago they celebrated Pompey's triumph. Now they celebrate the triumph of the one "that comes in triumph over Pompey's blood" (I.i.55). They throw their caps into the air the way the rabble of London celebrated Essex after his triumphal return following his victory over the Spanish Armada, and then once again when he was led to the scaffold. Shakespeare knew how to cut history according to cut-off heads. In *Julius Caesar* the cut of the reenacted history begins with the end of the first Triumvirate and the beginning of the autocracy and ends with the new autocracy of Octavius. Octavius gives the command for Brutus to be buried with all honors, but in the meantime he keeps Brutus's body in his own tent. But the new Caesar does not stop there. He continues: "So call the field to rest, and let's away, / To part the glories of this happy day" (V.v.80–81). The murder of Julius Caesar ends with "this happy day."

It is a strange ending for a tragedy. But *Hamlet*, written two years later, also ends in the same fashion. Fortinbras also gives the command for military honors to be paid to the body of the prince of Denmark. But he places himself on the Danish throne. "The rest is silence." No! The rest is Fortinbras. When Horatio attempts to talk about the prince in Ingmar Bergman's most recent unorthodox production of *Hamlet,* Fortinbras pulls out a revolver and shoots Horatio on the spot. Witnesses to the past are unneeded. It was likewise a "happy day" for Fortinbras. Bergman has made *Hamlet* contemporary. In Bergman's reading of *Hamlet,* history is its tragic hero. So it is in *Julius Caesar.*

3

For the twenty-two-year-old Georg Büchner *Julius Caesar* was the model of historical tragedy. But it was not a dead model. Or perhaps it could be put differently: for Büchner *Julius Caesar* was the model not of historical tragedy, but of the tragedy of history. For that reason Caesar's death could be updated once more and transposed in *Danton's Death* into the drama of revolution.

At a midnight meeting of the conspirators, Brutus says:

> Let's be sacrificers, but not butchers, Caius.
> We all stand up against the spirit of Caesar;
> And in the spirit of men there is no blood.
> . . . .
> Let's carve him as a dish fit for the gods,
> Not hew him as a carcase fit for hounds:
> . . . .
> . . . to the common eyes,
> We shall be call'd purgers, not murderers.
>
> (II.i.166ff.)

Brutus wants to put Caesar's body on the altar of the republic. Murder is to be changed into a ritual in which the sacrificial lamb is being sacrificed in order to save venerable Rome. "Let's be sacrificers, but not butchers." The spirit has no blood, but the sacrificial lamb bleeds. Shakespeare knew that ritual murder is still murder. The same pure Brutus who one hour before sunrise on the day of the murder had talked about Caesar's death as an act of cleansing, the way a surgeon talks about a pure operation with antiseptic gloves on, now when the deed is done lifts his bloody hands over Caesar's body. After the murder, there is born a new Brutus—an ideologue.

> And let us bathe our hands in Caesar's blood
> Up to the elbows, and besmear our swords:
> Then walk we forth even to the market place.
> (III.i. 105–7)

In *Danton's Death* Saint-Just, who at the meeting of the Committee of the Public Safety sits next to Robespierre, is the one to speak first. He repeats almost exactly Brutus's words, which Shakespeare took from Plutarch: "We must bury the great corpse with proper decorum, like priests, not murderers. We dare not chop it up, all its limbs must fall with it."[3] Robespierre interrupts him: "Speak more clearly." Büchner completes Shakespeare's unfinished thought. Now Saint-Just becomes a Cassius, who had demanded that Antony be done away with along with Caesar. "We must bury him in full armor and slaughter his horses and slaves on his burial mound" (I.vi).

Shakespeare's Brutus calls the murderers the purgers. In Büchner, Robespierre and Saint-Just draw up the list of names for the great purge of the Terror. One after the other, they list the deputies to the Convention, the Jacobins, the old comrades, including Camille Desmoulins, the legendary Vieux Cordelier and Robespierre's schoolmate and friend. He had dared to call the incorruptible the "Messiah of Blood." "Then quickly, tomorrow," says the new Brutus of the Revolution. "No long death agony! I've become sensitive lately. Quickly!" And Büchner adds, in the spirit of Macbeth: "Only the dead do not return." It turned out to be a ill-fated prophecy.

Büchner was not the first one to show how the French Revolution clothed itself in the costume of republican Rome, but he did it long before Marx. Even more penetratingly and more sharply than Marx, Büchner revealed for what sort of a masquerade and for what purpose that costume, and the Roman names and gestures, were intended. In scene ii of *Danton's Death,* as in Shakespeare, the action is switched to the streets. A drunken theater prompter mercilessly batters his wife while reciting some fragments from *Hamlet* and shouting at the passersby: "A knife, give me a knife, Romans!" He calls her alternately a whore or Baucis, and he calls his daughter Lucretia. This chaste Lucretia stands on the corner. "Would you have a pair of pants to pull *up,*" the new Baucis asks her husband, "if the young gentlemen didn't pull theirs *down* with her?"

In the street scene of *Julius Caesar* the Roman rabble, enraged by Caesar's murder, attacks Cinna the poet instead of Cinna the conspirator. His name happens to be the same! In the street scene of *Danton's Death* the citizens drag to the lamppost a passer-by who has a handkerchief around his neck. "Our wives and children cry out for bread. We want to feed them with the flesh of aristocrats. Hey! Kill anyone without a hole in his coat!"

Less than a year before writing *Danton's Death* Büchner founded in Giessen the clandestine Society for the Rights of Man, prepared the ground for the "revolution," and in *The Hessian Messenger (Der Hessische Landbote),* of which he was the publisher, declared, "Freedom for the huts! War to the palaces!" Now with all the bitterness and consciousness of the defeat, convinced of the implacable fatalism of history, and abandoning Schiller for Shakespeare (Schiller when he wrote *The Robbers* was almost two full years younger than Büchner), he did not forget that the people were hungry. It was the same in Hesse ruled by feudal princes as it had been in Paris during the Revolution. Instead of bread, revolution could offer only heads falling in the basket from the guillotine.

"The weapon of the Republic is terror, the power of the Republic is virtue. Virtue, for without it, terror is corruptible.

Terror, for without it, virtue is powerless." Büchner extracted from Robespierre's speeches the pure essence. One could say the acidic essence. In this reading of Robespierre, most striking is the oxymoron of revolution in which terror is virtue and virtue is terror. In *Danton's Death* Büchner was in all likelihood the first—a hundred years before Orwell—to unveil the newspeak of terror. "Terror is an outgrowth of virtue. . . . The revolutionary government is the despotism of freedom against the tyranny of Kings." In such a chilling semantics all terms can be inverted at will. Kindness turns into crime, and crime into kindness. "To punish the oppressors of mankind is kindness— to pardon them is barbarity." The despotism of freedom differs from the despotism of kings only by the heads that fell from the guillotine, just as internationalism differs from cosmopolitanism by the thousands who perished in Lubyanka prison or rotted in the labor camps. It is quite possible that Büchner found this chilling semantics not only in Robespierre but also in Shakespeare's Brutus. Consider Brutus's speech over Caesar's body:

> then is death a benefit:
> So are we Caesar's friends, that we have abridg'd
> His time of fearing death.
>
> (III.i. 103–5)

The horror of this stupefying sentence, which must be breathtaking if delivered by a great actor, became clear to me only through Büchner's Robespierre. "To punish the oppressors of mankind is kindness." But Büchner unveiled in Robespierre's speeches not only the semantics of terror but also its deadly logic as well. "The internal enemies of the Republic consist of two factions, like two armies." The relentless repetitious quality of this logic seems to be the very nature of terror. "One of these factions," Number One continues, "no longer exists. In its presumptuous insanity it tried to throw aside the most proven patriots as worn-out weaklings in order to rob the Republic of its strongest arms. It declared war on God and property in order to create a diversion on behalf of the kings. It parodied the illustrious drama of the Revolution in order to compromise it through premeditated excesses. Hébert's triumph would have turned the Republic into chaos, and despotism would have been satisfied. The sword of judgement has struck the traitor down." I do not think that it is necessary to modernize Robespierre's logic. Two factions, two deviations, but both are the enemies of the people. Let us carry this thought to its logical conclusion: terror produces enemies because enemies justify terror. The other faction "is the opposite of the first. It leads us to weakness; its battle cry is: mercy!" After the Trotskyites we have Zinovyev and the followers of Bukharin; after Hébert and the Hébertists we have Danton.

Then there is this brief exchange, which likewise needs no updating. We have all heard it too often.

> ROBESPIERRE: Whoever said that an innocent person was struck down?
> DANTON: Do you hear that, Fabricius? No innocent person was killed!

What is even more astonishing is that the twenty-two-year-old Büchner shows not only the logic of terror but the face of the incorruptible as well. Where did he learn that? Here again Büchner served his apprenticeship with Shakespeare. Sleep has abandoned Robespierre, just as it did Brutus that night full of "figures and fantasies" before the murder of Caesar, or Macbeth after killing the king. Robespierre is also *after*. He looks at Paris out of the opened window: "I can't tell what part of me is deceiving the other. Night snores over the earth and wallows in wild dreams. . . . Aren't we sleepwalkers?" At that moment, enter Saint-Just, the archangel of terror. A maid brings a lighted candelabra. Death sentences are being signed. Even the closest friends must perish. Robespierre is once more left alone. A new day breaks. From the window the guillotine erected at the Place de la Révolution can be seen. "They're all leaving me—all is desolate and empty—I am alone." Robespierre brushes off his jacket. From early childhood he hated dirt. His face is almost white. He has powdered it again. He smiles. I know this smile from hundreds of portraits of Stalin, and from Shakespeare as well: "O villain, villain, smiling, damned villain!" (*Hamlet* I.v.106).

4

In *Danton's Death* the guillotine appears onstage for the first time only at the denouement, but its presence can be felt from the beginning to the end. If I were to stage *Danton's Death*, the shadow of the guillotine would be present throughout the play. It would always be looming over the stage or the audience, over the actors and the spectators alike, since in this kind of theater the spectators become the actors.

In scene i the conversations take place to the accompaniment of cards being shuffled and falling on the card table. "Did it rain during the guillotining or did you get a bad seat and not see anything?" *The guillotining*. But who guillotined whom? *They* did, but who are *they*? Around the card table Hérault-Séchelles converses with Camille Desmoulins and Phillipeau. Danton sits nearby. All three are the deputies to the Convention. So who are *they*? The guillotiners or the guillotined? The game is being played with cards falling on the table like severed heads during the first week of April 1794. In Büchner's play as in Shakespeare's histories, time passes at variable speeds; only the hours of the day or night are given precisely. But historical dates are precise. In October 1793, during the trial of Marie

Antoinette, Hébert heaped abuse upon the queen and demanded her immediate execution. Six months later in the fourth week of March 1794, and hence not more than a week before that gathering around the card table, Danton sent Hébert to the guillotine. Not even an entire week later, or perhaps it was only three days after that rainy morning when Phillipeau got a bad seat at the Place de la Révolution and had difficulty seeing *the guillotining*, he was executed, along with Danton, Camille Desmoulins, and Hérault-Séchelles, at the same time of day. The difference was that now it was easier to see.

The spectators, those sending others to the guillotine, and the guillotined changed rapidly at the Place de la Révolution. The guillotine was called the "grand widow." "She has had at least a half-dozen husbands," Desmoulins wrote at an unguarded moment, "and she had to bury them all." "On couche avec, on ne la feconde pas," wrote Victor Hugo in *93*. ("Men lie with her, but she does not become pregnant.") On days when it stood idle, the guillotine was covered with a white sheet, like an altar. On this altar the Revolution rejuvenated itself with every new victim. "The Revolution is like the daughters of Pelias: it cuts humanity in pieces to rejuvenate it. Humanity will rise up with mighty limbs out of this cauldron of blood, like the earth out of the waters of the Flood, as if it had been newly created." At that point the deputies to the Convention gave Saint-Just a long, sustained standing ovation. At the same meeting of the Convention Saint-Just asked for Danton's head.

That same night, or perhaps it was the night before, neither Robespierre nor Danton was able to sleep. In this drama not only of history but also of those who must enact it, in this sudden dramatic kinship between Danton and Robespierre, Shakespeare's Brutus with his nightly specters is housed within both of them. Now it is Danton standing at the window looking out at Paris. He hears the voices coming from outside, or perhaps he hears them within himself: "September, September!" During the first days of September 1792, the sansculottes massacred thousands of prisoners in Paris and the provinces.

> JULIE: The Kings were just forty hours from Paris. . . .
> DANTON: We killed them. That was not murder, that was internal war.
> JULIE: You saved the country.

"The guillotine is an instrument of division," writes the contemporary French historian François Furet, "separating the good from the bad."[4] It should be added that by means of this instrument of division the good would invariably turn into the bad, and patriots would turn into traitors. In this theater of revolution, we and *they*, spectators, those sending others to the guillotine and the guillotined, all change places, sometimes in the course of one week. Rather than the division proposed by Furet, I prefer the one expressed by the executioner in Stanisław Jerzy Lec's *Unkempt Thoughts*: "You can divide people in many ways. Said the astonished executioner: 'I just divide them into heads and bodies.' "[5]

The guillotine is the image, sign, and symbol of revolutionary terror. But all three of these characterizations are quite abstract. The Shakespearean Wheel of Fortune is indicated by the heads of rebels on London Bridge, leading across the Thames. Feudal history set this Grand Mechanism in motion, and although the steps leading to the throne can be represented onstage, the Grand Mechanism is only a theorem. The guillotine is not a theorem. Two or three times a week throughout the entire year of 1793 until Thermidor 1794, the tumbrils would leave La Conciergerie for the Place de la Révolution, the heads of the condemned sticking out like pinecones. The great painter David watched the tumbrils going by from the windows of his studio, and he sketched Marie Antoinette on her way to the guillotine. He also drew the cut-off heads in order to capture their final grimaces. David was a great realist.

The Capitol was the "chronotope" of Caesarism since the murder of Julius Caesar. "Dum Capitolium scandet cum tacita virgine pontifex." In Bakhtin's terminology, the chronotope of the Terror was the Place de la Révolution. "The Revolution is like Saturn, it devours its own children." In this sentence, so often quoted, the reference to Saturn is striking. Saturn/Chronos devoured his own offspring in order to stop time. The Revolution, compared with Saturn, has no end in sight. It is the permanent revolution. Trotsky was the great spokesman for the "permanent Revolution." The guillotine is the image and instrument of this permanent revolution.

The "Grand Veuve" is almost a character, as though it demanded victims. In *Danton's Death* the guillotine cuts off Danton's head; in actual history, less than six months after Danton's execution, it cut off Robespierre's head. In Büchner's play the guillotine is the third protagonist of the drama, along with Danton and Robespierre. According to Aristotle, tragedy is the fall of a great man, the destruction of values. In Büchner's play the guillotine is a tragic hero. It destroyed the Revolution that it was supposed to save. The "Fearsome Widow" has two faces: that of a savior and that of an executioner.

In the last scene of *Danton's Death*, the day after the execution, the widow of Camille Desmoulins, who was executed along with Danton, sits on the steps of the guillotine:

LUCILE: *(Reflectively, then suddenly as if reaching a decision)*
Long live the King!
CITIZEN: In the name of the Republic! *(She is surrounded by the watch and is led off.)*

5

Tragedy is the cutting off of a historical sequence. In *Danton's Death* the action starts a week, or perhaps only a few days, before Danton's execution. But the dates mentioned in the play refer to the events that took place earlier. They are enumerated by Saint-Just: "the 14th of July, the 10th of August, the 31st of May." The storming of the Bastille, the dethroning of Louis XVI, the seizure of power by the Jacobins: Saint-Just is enumerating the key dates of the Revolution. There are two other important dates, both in September 1792: the massacre of the prisoners and the proclamation of the Republic. But where in *Danton's Death* is the final cutting off of history?

Lucile's suicidal scream ends act IV. *Danton's Death* has no act V. In the entire history of theater, starting with Greek tragedy, which is divided into five episodes, through the Renaissance and up to the German and French Romantics, I know of no instance of a drama in four acts that has left its mark. There always have been three acts or five acts. What happened to act V in Büchner?

Roman Jakobson calls the absence of a foot or a part of it at the end of a line of verse a zero sign. That sign signifies. It signifies an absence. Barthes has written about the sign that is nonpresence. A letter that has not arrived is such a sign of nonpresence. A dead telephone is also such a sign. He did not call; she did not call. He did not write. She did not write. In a theatrical performance, a nonpresent, nonexistent, *nonwritten* act V goes on existing as an expectation. It is a present continuation, only suspended. In tragedy it is a nonfinished tragedy. In historical drama it is history still open and also as though suspended.

In *Danton's Death* Robespierre's execution is foreshadowed or rather foretold. During the final night before his execution

Danton says to his fellow prisoners: "Freedom will now re-
spectably prostitute herself in the marriage bed of the lawyer of
Arras. But I imagine she'll play Clytemnestra to him. I don't
give him six months. I'm dragging him down with me."
    This nonexistent act V could have been Robespierre's exe-
cution. The cutting out of the history being reenacted would
have started with the destruction of the Bastille, or at least with
the September massacres, and would have ended with Thermidor. *Danton's Death* then could have had an ending nearly
comparable to the denouement of *Julius Caesar:* "Take away the
corpses and let soldiers bivouac at the Place de la Révolution,"
says the future First Consul, still wearing his general's uniform,
white, tightly fitting trousers and the three-cornered hat of the
revolutionary army. But he has already put his hand over his
breast in celebration of his first victory. "So call the field to
rest, and let's away, / To part the glories of this happy day" (*Julius Caesar* V.v.80–81).
    The guillotine in its wagon faithfully accompanied Napo-
leon's army in all the campaigns until the very last. "Politics is
destiny," said Napoleon. In 1808, during the meeting of European monarchs in Erfurt, on hearing Goethe's praise of
Voltaire's *Mahomet* as an example of *Schicksal-tragödie*, the em-
peror interrupted: "Tragedy of destiny? But now it belongs to
the past. Politics is *das Schicksal.*"
    In the nonexistent act V of *Danton's Death*, history contin-
ues to move ahead, constantly digging like Shakespeare's mole:
"old mole. . . . / A worthy pioner!" (*Hamlet* I.v.170–71). Its
conclusion was not Thermidor, the end of the Reign of Terror
and the beginning of Caesarism. For Büchner the time of the
Terror did not end with the cutting off of Robespierre's head.
In that nonwritten act V of *Danton's Death*, this chapter of history continues to be a bitter affair. When will it end? With what
sort of new defeat after what kind of new revolution?

"Long live the King! In the name of the Republic!" After the demise of the July Revolution, the Bourbon fleurs-de-lis did not return to adorn the coat of the king of France. France became a bourgeois monarchy with *le Roi-citoyen* on the throne. For the first readers of *Danton's Death* in the mid-1830s, and even for the first spectators in 1902, Lucile's suicidal scream on the steps of the scaffold contained a sinister irony. Kings were already reigning "in the name of the Republic." This nonexistent act V still goes on, still keeps being played, *le temps des assasins*, the time of uninterrupted terror.

There are always two ways to interpret historical drama: comparing it with the historical time it reenacts and recalling the historical time in which it was written. It has been repeatedly pointed out that there are two different Dantons in Büchner's play: the historical Danton with a lion's mane who proclaimed the death of monarchy on 10 August 1792, then twice mobilized the people of Paris against the interventionist army threatening the capital, the most fiery orator at the Convention and the Jacobins clubs, and the other Danton, who could pass for an alter ego of Büchner's, when his attempt to incite Hesse to revolt failed and ended in personal disaster. His closest friends were arrested, and Büchner first sought refuge in Darmstadt. Less than a month after finishing *Danton's Death*, he crossed the border without a passport and began his life as an émigré in Strasbourg. In France *le Roi-citoyen* had been on the throne for five years.

"I was finally bored with it all." Is it possible to imagine a Danton who is "bored with it all" during the Reign of Terror? "I'm not lazy, just tired. The soles of my feet are on fire!" A tired Danton! Again in the same act he says to his friends: "What's the difference if they die under the guillotine or from a fever or from old age?" He continues, "Life isn't worth the effort we make to maintain it." Once again this Danton speaks from a different, alien century: "A mistake was made when we were created—something is missing. I have no name for it." The young genius who, after writing *Danton's Death* in five weeks, less than a year later at Zurich University defended his doctoral thesis on the nervous system of the barbel, a small fish frequently encountered in the lakes around Giessen, personified all the contradictions of his time at an astonishing level of concentration, one might even say approaching a paroxysm. He wrestled with the tradition of German idealism, and he went far beyond Goethe in his thesis on the small fish, which, according to some commentators, was a forecast of Darwin. Born nine years after Feuerbach and three years before Marx, Büchner was an implacable materialist terrified by the fatalism of history. "We haven't made Revolution; the Revolution has made us."

Danton/Büchner remains an ardent revolutionary even after the defeat, even after the many defeats of his own revolution, the Revolution of 1830, and of that abortive German rebellion in Hesse in 1833. But this alter ego of twenty-two-year-old Büchner is projected even further into the future. Danton seems to be a forerunner of modern existential despair: "The world is chaos. Nothingness is the world-god yet to be born. . . . Nothingness has killed itself, Creation is its wound, we are its drops of blood, the world is the grave in which it rots." Then there is this astonishing quotation, which could come from Beckett's *Endgame*, in the mouth of this totally unexpected twentieth-century Danton: "Death apes birth: dying we're just as helpless and naked as newborn children. Indeed, our shroud is our diaper. We can whimper in the grave as well as in the cradle."

Great texts, great dramas always have this double way of being contemporary: for their own time and for the time in which they are read or staged anew. Yet in some amazing way, which for me will be forever mysterious, it is as though these texts were conversing with other texts that they could not possibly know or rather whose authors could not even have heard of one another. "The Revolution is like Saturn, it devours its own children." In the same year, 1835, when Büchner wrote his *Danton's Death*, or perhaps even a year earlier or later—the dating is still not certain—Adam Mickiewicz, who was in Paris or perhaps already in Lausanne, jotted down in the margin of another poem in an almost illegible handwriting the following:

> Names dear to the people the people will forget
> All will pass away; after thunder, roaring, and toil
> The inheritance will be seized by dim-witted, dense, petty man.

At that time Mickiewicz was living in Lausanne, so if the poem were written in 1836, he would have been no more than a hundred miles away from Büchner in Zurich.

6

Almost twenty years after the execution of Marie Antoinette, and still twenty years before Büchner's *Danton's Death*, a spot was excavated in the center of Paris—not far from what is today the Boulevard Haussmann—in which the victims of the guillotine were buried. This common grave contained more than three hundred bodies. It was possible to identify almost all of them. As Kazimierz Brandys pointed out in his *Months*, among those discovered there were Danton and Charlotte Corday, Madame Roland, Philippe Egalité, Lavoisier, and Camille Desmoulins and his wife, Lucile, who in Büchner's play screamed on the steps of the guillotine: "Long live the King!" The remains of the royal couple were also found and at a later point were transferred by the Bourbons to Saint-Denis.

Büchner never stopped hating kings. Likewise, his Danton said on the night preceding his execution: "The flood of the

Revolution can discharge our corpses wherever it wants; they'll still be able to beat in the skulls of all kings with our fossilized bones." *Danton's Death* is a drama of historical despair. But in this despair there is still some hope—not totally extinguished, but embittered. "If history ever opens its graves, despotism can still suffocate from the stench of our bodies."

For me this hope held by Danton/Büchner is akin to Nadezhda Mandelstam's "hope against hope," or perhaps to Camus's "hope full of despair" and "despair full of hope," which has been my only consolation for many years.

Notes

1. John Webster, *The Duchess of Malfi*, New Mermaid edition, ed. E. M. Brennan (Harlow, Essex, 1987).

2. Quotations of Shakespeare are from the Arden Shakespeare editions: *Julius Caesar*, ed. T. S. Dorsch (London, 1977); *Hamlet*, ed. Harold Jenkins (London, 1982).

3. Georg Büchner, *Danton's Death*, trans. Henry J. Schmidt (New York, 1971). All quotations are from this translation.

4. François Furet, *Penser la Revolution française* (Paris, 1978), 115.

5. Stanislaw Jerzy Lec, *Unkempt Thoughts,* trans. Jacek Galazka (New York, 1962), 47.

Translated by Jadwiga Kosicka

APPENDIX

Directors and the Ghost

S hakespeare scholars have always been uneasy about the Ghost in *Hamlet*. They have never been sure whether it came from hell or purgatory, or according to what system of theology, Protestant or Catholic, it returned errant on earth, or how much the student of philosophy just back from Wittenberg could trust it. But directors have even greater troubles with the Ghost. The dramatic function of the Ghost is important, but even more important is the question What should the Ghost look like? Like a ghost, but what does a ghost look like? The Ghost of the dead king is supposed not only to frighten the sentinels on the battlements and Horatio but also to arouse a feeling of dread in the audience or at least not to provoke laughter. A Ghost in rusted armor that clinks at every step cannot be taken seriously. But how else can it be presented? In Peter Hall's production of *Hamlet* that took place some twenty years ago, the actor playing the Ghost sat on the shoulders of a hidden extra who rode on a bicycle. This gave the impression that the Ghost was swimming silently through space. The *onnagata* playing the role of a geisha in the Japanese Kabuki theater glides in a similar fashion. After a few moments, though, the audience caught on to Peter Hall's trick, and laughter accompanied the bicycle-riding Ghost to the end of the scene. Of course, there are other ways of doing it. I have seen a Ghost on stilts and an Italian Ghost—projected on a screen at the back of the stage—that was Hamlet's enlarged shadow lighted from underneath. But even this shadow that spoke with an amplified voice did little to make the Ghost convincing to me.

The most spectacular Ghost was one I saw in a French production that came to Berlin in the early fall of 1989. The performances took place in a huge sports hall with an enormous arenalike stage. The Ghost, clad in full armor, made his entrance on horseback. The horse trotted, galloped, and at one point almost trampled Hamlet, Horatio, and the soldiers. The idea of showing the Ghost galloping on a horse undoubtedly came from the Romantic Cirque Olympique.

So perhaps the Ghost does not have to look like a ghost at all. Perhaps it should appear as the dead do in our dreams. That was how it was presented more than ten years ago when Jonathan Miller showed his *Hamlet* in New York with a group of students from Oxford and Cambridge. It was in no way amateur theater. It was one of the most penetrating analytical productions of *Hamlet* that I have ever seen. The actors looked as though they had just stepped out of a court painting by Velázquez. They all wore the same black costumes with enormous white ruffs. So did Hamlet. The Ghost appeared in the same black outfit, with a white ruff and a black peaked hat with a broad brim. There was a small bench by the proscenium on which the Ghost sat with Hamlet and conversed with him as father with son. The Ghost put his arm around Hamlet's shoulders and explained everything. Very considerately. As though it were an ordinary conversation. And the ordinariness of the conversation with the Ghost was deeply moving.

In a recent cinematic adaptation of Hamlet directed by Franco Zeffirelli, the Ghost, who appears on the terrace of an authentic Gothic castle, apparently somewhere in Scotland, is an "ordinary" Ghost, wearing neither armor nor a helmet and visor. The only unusual happening is that at times the Ghost, dimly outlined against the castle's walls and the sea, seems to dissolve into the air. Only a great actor like Paul Scofield could show the "noble father" in an "ordinary Ghost" and convey all the horror of the violent death and suffering of that "noble Ghost."

In his never-realized *Hamlet* in Kraków, Konrad Swinarski had intended to go back to the traditional image of the Ghost. We know how the Ghost was supposed to look from a conversation with the set designers, Lidia and Jerzy Skarżyński, which was faithfully recorded by Józef Opalski. The Ghost was not only to have been encased in armor, but beneath this armor his body was to have been visible, "putrefying, with pulsating abscesses." "A cheap trick on the part of the old Ghost," the Skarżyńskis say, undoubtedly repeating Swinarski's own words, "designed to affect his naive young son and incite him to vengeance." In this conception, the Ghost—a putrefying corpse in armor—was to be the embodiment of the feudal wars of plunder waged by old Hamlet, which the cautious Claudius, following a new policy of pragmatic diplomacy, had abandoned. *Pace* Swinarski! We need not always have blind faith in the theorizing of even the most brilliant director. But Swinarski had an astonishing and penetrating intuition about another role for the Ghost: the Ghost as an evocation of the past, as an appeal that it never be forgotten.

Something like that happened about ten years ago. I saw a production of *Hamlet* in Dubrovnik. It was in August. Dubrovnik was baked white by the sun. The old town is surrounded by walls. They shut out the sea at almost every point. The small rocky beaches are located outside the town. In the town itself, among the walls scorched white in the sun, one has menacing feelings of claustrophobia, as though there were no place to escape to. One continually meets the same faces and hears the same voices. Even in the evenings, once the relentless heat has abated, the white walls of the houses still radiate the feverish heat. Well into the early hours of the morning the narrow streets resound with broken cries in assorted languages. Dubrovnik at night is a gathering place for seagulls. In Dalmatian slang "seagulls" are boys who sell their love.

In Dubrovnik, right outside the old town, there is an old castle half in ruins. Every summer *Hamlet* is presented in this castle. Often, given the surroundings, these productions are quite extraordinary. I particularly remember one such *Hamlet* that I saw some ten years ago. The performances began late in the evening in the courtyard of the castle, where wooden benches were set up in front of a simple platform made of planks. When the royal court appeared on the platform, it seemed for a moment as if the spectators had left their benches and come up on the stage. Gertrude and Claudius wore brightly colored coats, a cross between beach and evening wear, and looked as though they had just stepped into one of the innumerable Dubrovnik *gostinica* (restaurants) for the local specialty: grilled *raznici* and a bottle of red wine. Ophelia was barefoot and wearing the then-fashionable red bikini, her small round breasts almost completely exposed. The ladies-in-waiting and courtiers looked as though they had been unexpectedly transported from a Venetian carnival to Dubrovnik in the middle of summer. When the stage grew empty, the Ghost appeared at the top of a flight of crumbling stairs in a niche in the wall. He was wearing a striped concentration camp uniform. His "Adieu, adieu! Hamlet, remember me," echoed throughout the ruins of the castle. Yet his cry remained suspended in the void. The Ghost in the striped uniform bathed in the spotlights seemed to be a specter from the past—from the past that everyone in Dubrovnik/Elsinore wanted to forget forever.

The Ghost was not the only guest who arrived at the castle on the third day after the marriage of the new king to his elder brother's freshly made widow. Hamlet was likewise a stranger in this new court of magnificent European holiday festivities. In his black cape Hamlet too appeared to be an anachronistic specter of dead ideologies amid the spectators and actors who even at that late hour in the evening seemed equally heated by the midday sun and by the wine. The sarcastic remarks of that lean and long-haired dissident from Wittenberg sounded hopelessly out of place, and his complaints that the time was out of joint and that he was born to set it right seemed uncalled-for arrogance. There were no Hamlets in the audience in Dubrovnik.

In both Jonathan Miller's production more than ten years ago and in Swinarski's *Hamlet*, which had reached the final rehearsals, the same actor played the Ghost and Fortinbras. For me the reasons for such doubling in casting were neither clear nor convincing. But with the passing of time I have learned to trust directors more than Shakespeare scholars. Since the time of young Goethe and then the German and French Romantics, through the naturalists, modernists, and decadents both early and late, Hamlet has been not only the central character in drama but also always someone contemporary. In Hamlet they discovered their own traits, their own hopes, defeats, and despair. All the other characters in the tragedy were not only secondary; they were purely historical. But in the last decade, and maybe even somewhat earlier, directors have been paying closer and closer attention to the significance of the Ghost and Fortinbras, perhaps not only because in the logic of action and structure the tragedy at Elsinore begins with the arrival of the Ghost and ends with the departure of Fortinbras. With increasing urgency the Ghost and Fortinbras appear as signs of history—and not only the history of Elsinore, but the history that already has happened and could happen again. A few years after seeing the Dubrovnik Ghost in the striped concentration camp uniform I saw *Hamlet* at the National Theatre in London, with the Ghost in a long World War I trench coat coming down to the ground, riddled with bullet holes. In another *Hamlet*, also British, Fortinbras's bodyguard wore armbands with swastikas. Such extreme "modernizations" are probably intrusive and unwarranted. But for the contemporary director the Ghost and Fortinbras are once again *ante portas*.

Bergman's Swedish *Hamlet*, shown briefly in New York a few years back, ends in a glare of lights and the buzzing of television sets. Fortinbras's soldiers pile the corpses one on top of the other and count them. Methodically. As if they were clearing a battlefield. Everyone has forgotten about Hamlet. No one bears off his body. In *Hamlet* as planned by Swinarski, troops were to gather on Szczepanski Square in front of the Stary Theater before the performance. Then in the last scene they were to invade not only the stage but also the auditorium from all sides, coming through all the doors and through the windows facing the square, and coming down on ropes from the balconies onto the heads of the spectators.

"The rest is silence." The end is not Hamlet's silence, but the deafening drums of Fortinbras's troops.

Translated by Jadwiga Kosicka

Index